FACEBOOK ADS MADE SIMPLE

How to Create High-Converting Facebook Ads in an Hour or Less

ANDREA VAHL

First edition

Go Big Productions
Louisville, Colorado, USA

Print edition
ISBN 978-0-692-19944-2

Edited and proofed by Brit McGinnis

ADVANCE PRAISE FOR FACEBOOK ADS MADE SIMPLE

"Andrea Vahl has been a Facebook pro since the beginning. She's takes the complex topic of Facebook ads and makes it easy to understand. That's why she's been teaching at Social Media Marketing World since the start. If you want to master Facebook ads, pick up this book. You won't regret it."

— MICHAEL STELZNER, FOUNDER OF SOCIAL MEDIA EXAMINER

"Andrea Vahl is the entire internet's smart, go-to source for Facebook Ads. And now she's collected all her wisdom in this actionable book. So now she's smart AND generous!"

— ANN HANDLEY, CHIEF CONTENT OFFICER OF MARKETINGPROFS

"Running Facebook ads without reading this guide is like making an omelette without turning on a stove: it's doable, but you're setting yourself up for sadness, frustration, and time-wasting. Before you spend one more penny with Facebook, please learn from Andrea Vahl."

— JAY BAER, FOUNDER OF CONVINCE & CONVERT AND CO-AUTHOR OF *TALK TRIGGERS*

"You've been told you need to advertise on Facebook but where do you start?

There are a lot of ways you can waste your money on Facebook like boosting bad posts, wrong targeting, bad optimization but luckily Andrea Vahl has you covered. In this book, Facebook Ads Made Simple, *she not only walks you through the best tactics and strategies but tells you WHY Facebook Ads work the way they do so you can make the best decisions for your business.*

I highly recommend this book for anyone looking to get the best results from their Facebook Ads!"

— LARRY KIM, CEO OF MOBILEMONKEY, INC., AND FOUNDER OF WORDSTREAM, ONE OF THE WORLD'S LARGEST FACEBOOK AD AGENCIES

"Ok, let's be honest — nothing about Facebook Ads is easy! But Andrea Vahl does a masterful job of breaking down all the moving parts, and truly does make understanding — but more importantly — using Facebook Ads more simple. Also, Andrea is funny. And that goes a long way in making her content more digestible. If you are looking for a good book to get you started in using — or to make you more success with employing Facebook Ads — then buy this one!!!"

— VIVEKA VON ROSEN, LINKEDIN EXPERT AND AUTHOR

"Facebook ads can be overwhelming for small business owners. I know — I've talked to thousands of them about it. This book will make it much easier for you to create effective ads. An excellent read, I give it two huge Likeable thumbs up!"

— DAVE KERPEN, FOUNDER, LIKEABLE MEDIA

CONTENTS

INTRODUCTION

Facebook is the largest social network on the web and represents a huge opportunity for your business. I've helped businesses have 6-figure launches, sell out events, double their referrals, get more foot traffic, grow their email list to 50k subscribers, sell online products, book more sales calls, sell homes, and so much more. I've been running ads for clients and for myself since 2010 and Facebook ads have changed a LOT in that time. But what hasn't changed is the fact that Facebook ads are extremely effective for helping businesses grow.

But you need to have a plan and a strategy for using Facebook ads effectively. Some people try one ad on Facebook and then when it doesn't work the way they want, they decide that Facebook ads are a waste of time.

Maybe you've been there yourself. While this book is titled "Facebook Ads Made Simple", I'm not suggesting that there isn't some work involved in methodically testing your ads. So don't get discouraged if your first one or two or ten ads don't work the way you hoped. Just continue to make progress towards that perfect combination of targeting, images, text, and call-to-action and you will have success!

Let's have a little fun, shall we?

One thing that I want you to know about me before we begin this journey together is that I like to have a little fun and use some humor. I started blogging as a slightly cranky character named Grandma Mary, Social Media Edutainer, back in 2009. (Most likely scarring my children but it was worth it.) That decision was instrumental to my business growth and led to the opportunity to co-author *Facebook Marketing All-in-One for Dummies* with Amy Porterfield and Phyllis Khare. Learning is more fun when you are laughing and Facebook can be challenging sometimes so you need to laugh.

WHO CAN BENEFIT FROM THIS BOOK

This book is designed for people just starting to use Facebook ads. You may be a complete beginner, or you may have already run a few Facebook ads and want to make sure you are on the right path. Either way, this book is for you. The Facebook ads platform has some extremely advanced tactics for the power user and those won't be covered in this book. I will give you some retargeting tactics and measurement techniques to take your ads farther but I encourage you to either take my full Facebook Ads course (at https://fbadvertisingsecrets.com/opennow) or follow my blog (www.andreavahl.com/blog) for more advanced training.

To get the most out of this book, you do need to have some familiarity with Facebook and preferably have a Facebook Page already set up for your business. A Facebook Page is necessary to advertise on Facebook.

A WORD ABOUT INSTAGRAM ADVERTISING

Instagram is owned by Facebook and uses the exact same "Ads Manager" platform to create ads. Any time I'm talking about Facebook ads in this book, the same concepts work for Instagram ads. Cool!

I have a section in the book specifically addressing Instagram ads because there are unique considerations when advertising on Instagram. The ads look different and there are some design changes you need to make when setting up your Instagram ad. As with anything I mention, you need to test the Instagram placement for yourself to see if your business can benefit from Instagram ads.

FACEBOOK IS CONSTANTLY CHANGING

As you may have noticed already, Facebook is always changing. I was considering titling this book "Who moved my button?" but I thought it wasn't quite specific enough. Facebook is always testing and tweaking what works best for their audience, and for the marketers that use their platform. Which is great from an innovation standpoint but not as good for authors and trainers hoping to teach people how to use the platform. On top of that, Facebook tends to roll changes out at different rates to different people. At any given moment, screens can look completely different for different people.

So I ask you to be be patient as you go through the book and refer to the screenshots. They may not look exactly the way you see them online. Typically the ideas and concepts are the same, but the menu items and button locations may be slightly different. Usually, if you look around the screen a little or dive a little deeper into one of the menus, you will find what you need. The concepts for testing your ads and determining your results are the same across any advertising platform.

CREATING HIGH-CONVERTING ADS IN AN HOUR OR LESS

Was the subtitle of this book compelling to you? I hope so! Was I lying? NO. Ok, I know you have to take some time to read the book and learn some new skills, so there is a little learning curve at the beginning.

I'm also not counting some of the initial setup you might have to do like installing your Facebook Pixel which just happens one time.

But creating high-converting ads is possible in a short amount of time. Here's a quick overview of the hour you will spend creating your ad and I'll cover each of these in detail in the book:

- 15 minutes - Research your Keywords

- 10 minutes - Create your Image
- 15 minutes - Writing your copy
- 10 minutes - Creating your Campaign, Ad Set, and Ad
- 10 minutes - Split testing another Ad

You may be a little slower than this to start but you will get faster!

BEYOND THE BOOK - A FREEBIE FOR YOU!

As Facebook continues to evolve and as your Facebook strategy evolves, you can keep up to date with the latest tips, news, and tactics on my blog: www.andreavahl.com/blog, and on my Facebook Page: www.facebook.com/AndreaVahlinc.

You can also get a FREE walk through video and other resources that will help with this book at www.andreavahl.com/book-resources Here is do a live demo of setting up an ad from scratch and give you pointers along the way of settings you need to change and what you can ignore. Plus I show you EXACTLY how to create the ad in an hour or less :)

If you want to really dive deep into Facebook Ads and get a year of online support in my private Facebook Group, you can join my Facebook Advertising Secrets course at https://fbadvertisingsecrets.com/opennow. This course has 2 levels - one for any type of business looking to learn how to use Facebook ads to grow their business (the Basic Level) and then also a level for people who want to build a business running Facebook Ads for clients (the Agency level). I only open the course a few times a year so you can visit the page and get on the waiting list (plus get a free Facebook Ads mini-course).

Thanks so much for starting your Facebook Ads journey with me! I appreciate you taking the time to invest in your success and learn a new skill. I know it can be uncomfortable to learn a new skill but I hope this book makes it SIMPLE for you!

1

WHY USE FACEBOOK ADS?

For marketers, Facebook has become a "pay-to-play" site.

You most likely don't need to be "sold" on the idea of Facebook advertising - since you have already purchased this book. But, JUST in case you need a little more convincing (or you need some ideas to help sell the boss on Facebook Ads), here are some of the top reasons businesses should use Facebook Ads.

#1 POSTING TO YOUR FACEBOOK PAGE ISN'T ENOUGH ANYMORE

Facebook is limiting "organic reach" of Facebook Pages. Organic reach is the number of people who see your content without paid distribution. For example, when you post an update on your Page, only a portion of your Fans see that post. Facebook will tell you exactly how many people saw the post in the "Insights" section which shows all the statistics for your Page.

Facebook has an algorithm to determine what is displayed to each user in the News Feed. The algorithm is based on many factors such as how often people interact with content from certain other people, how many people are commenting or interacting with the content, how recent the content is, and how many possible pieces of content are available to show someone. For example, if someone has a lot of friends posting regularly, then there are a lot of possible pieces of content to put into their News Feed. Or, if you are like my mom who has 5 friends on Facebook, then there isn't as much possible content to display.

Pages used to get more organic reach but Facebook made announcements in 2018 that they are focusing on personal profiles getting seen more rather than posts from Pages. https://newsroom.fb.com/news/2018/01/news-feed-fyi-bringing-people-closer-together/

In this image, the post reach of a popular Facebook Page is clearly in decline from January 1st, 2017 through February 22nd, 2018.

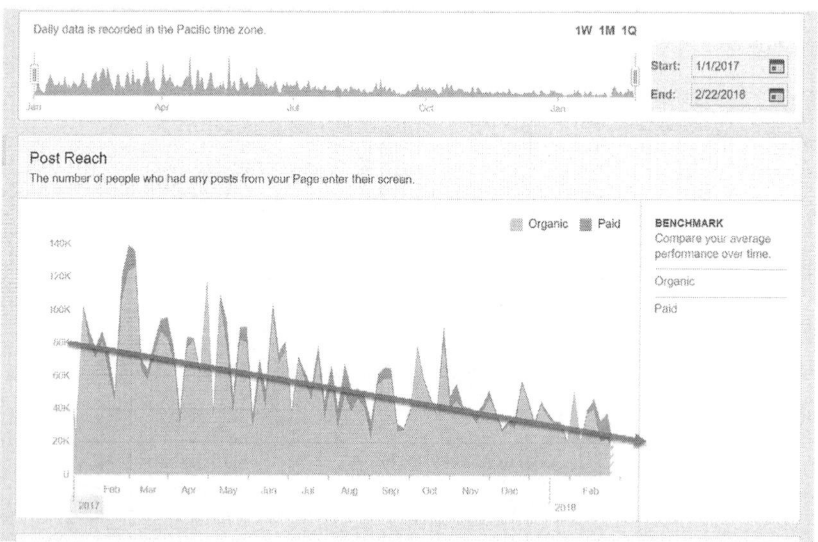

Unfortunately, there isn't too much we can do to control the reach that Facebook gives to Pages. To combat this decline in reach, it's necessary to spend a little money on Facebook ads.

The bottom line is that our Facebook Page content isn't getting seen for free as much anymore. Facebook needs to generate income in order to support the 25,000 people who work there - wow, that's like a small city! They generate income by running ads, and businesses have to pay for their content to be seen more.

#2 FACEBOOK IS STILL THE PLACE TO BE

Many people wonder if they should even bother with Facebook anymore as a marketing outlet. But people are still spending a LOT of time on Facebook. Facebook has **over 2.2 Billion users and 1.47 Billion people log into Facebook daily** as of June 2018. https://newsroom.fb.com/company-info/

While Facebook doesn't release the average time people spend on Facebook each day, many calculations suggest the average user spends between 30-50 minutes a day hanging out there. Whoa! That's a LOT of work-avoidance, right there.

Some people are concerned about the privacy scandals, fake news and the issues with election-meddling affecting ad performance. Facebook is taking these issues very seriously and wants to try and keep the users of the platform happy. As long as people continue to use Facebook regularly, Facebook is a great place for advertisers. Once people start leaving then it may be time to shift your strategy. Also, Instagram is continuing to see good growth and any of the advertising tactics in this book also apply to

Instagram - you are getting two-for-one learning here! No extra charge :)

If your audience is younger or truly not hanging out on Facebook, then maybe you need to consider other marketing avenues. But I've seen Facebook ads work for all types of businesses - authors, speakers, realtors, ecommerce, B2B (business-to-business), B2C (business-to-consumer), restaurants, insurance, mortgage brokers, healthcare, travel, online courses, local events, and more. I've had clients who had a larger following on Instagram than Facebook but the Facebook ads performed better than their Instagram ads. My message is to test Facebook ads against other types of marketing that might make sense so that you can compare for yourself what works best for your business.

#3 FACEBOOK ADS ARE HIGHLY TARGETED AND EASILY TRACKABLE

Other forms of advertising, such as newspapers, radio ads, tv ads, and magazine ads, aren't as effective anymore. These forms of advertising also aren't very trackable unless you have some type of exclusive coupon code just for that medium. Plus you are advertising to a very wide range of people with each of those ad placements.

With Facebook advertising you can select that you want to only advertise to the people who have indicated that they are interested in very specific things, such as Jogging or Yoga. You can also, in some cases, advertise to the fans of specific Facebook Pages like Runner's World, or Goat Yoga Today (Ok, I'm making that last Page up, but it's a real thing here in Boulder).

And you can select your demographics more precisely to advertise to people in, say, a certain zip code, within an age range, who are recently engaged, or have specific job titles. When you target your ads to your best demographic then you don't have to spend as much to reach that group and they will respond well to your ad.

With a tactic called "retargeting" that we will dive into later in this book, you can target your ads only to the people who have visited your website or watched your Facebook videos, for example. Retargeting is a powerful technique that gets you,in front of your "warm" audience who is already familiar with you and also lets you save money on your ads. Yeeha! Who doesn't love saving money??

#4 FACEBOOK IS ONE OF THE CHEAPEST PLACES TO ADVERTISE ONLINE

Speaking of saving money, Facebook is one of the cheapest places to advertise online. It can be cheaper than Google Adwords, LinkedIn ads, and Twitter Ads. Before my statistics purists jump all over this statement, let me say that I know that this is tough to qualify because there are a LOT of factors in this statement including location, industry, time of year, type of ad, etc. BUT I have looked at a lot of statistics and Facebook often skews lower than the other sites.

You definitely should do your own research and testing for your business. For example, for some businesses I've worked with, LinkedIn advertising yielded better conversions even though the cost per click is typically in the $5-10 range!

#5 PEOPLE NEED TO SEE YOUR OFFER MULTIPLE TIMES IN ORDER TO MAKE A BUYING DECISION

Reaching new potential customers and clients in any industry is a big factor in growing a business, obviously. But you can't expect a cold audience to be sold in an instant. Various studies show that people need to see an offer 5 times, or 7 times, or 20 times before deciding to pull out their wallet and buy. Facebook and Instagram advertising can help you get in front of your potential customers for less.

Hopefully this list got you even MORE excited about using Facebook Ads for your business. Facebook ads feel like a "gamble" sometimes. Maybe you've tried Facebook ads before and you didn't feel like they worked that well for you. Or maybe you had no idea how to even figure out what happened.

The good news is that you are in the right place by choosing this book! When you understand your strategy and put together a test plan, you will get better results from your Facebook Ads. There is a LOT to learn about Facebook ads but we'll start simple and give you more advanced strategies later in this book.

Let's get started! Charge!

Don't forget to grab your FREE live demo video and other resources that will help with this book at www.andreavahl.com/book-resources

2

HOW FACEBOOK ADS WORK

In this section, you will learn some of the ins and outs of how Facebook Ads work from a high level. In later sections of the book, I will go into more depth about these concepts and terms.

Facebook ads appear in many places on Facebook such as the News feed, the side bar, in the Messenger, in Instant Articles, and in videos. You can also use the Instagram placement option to place ads on Instagram from Facebook's interface. Facebook also has something called the "Audience Network," which is actually OFF of Facebook and on other websites and Apps that Facebook has partnered with to display ads. You will know the content is a Facebook ad when you see a "Sponsored" message, usually right below the Facebook Page name or at the top of posts in the ads on the right sidebar (as shown in this image).

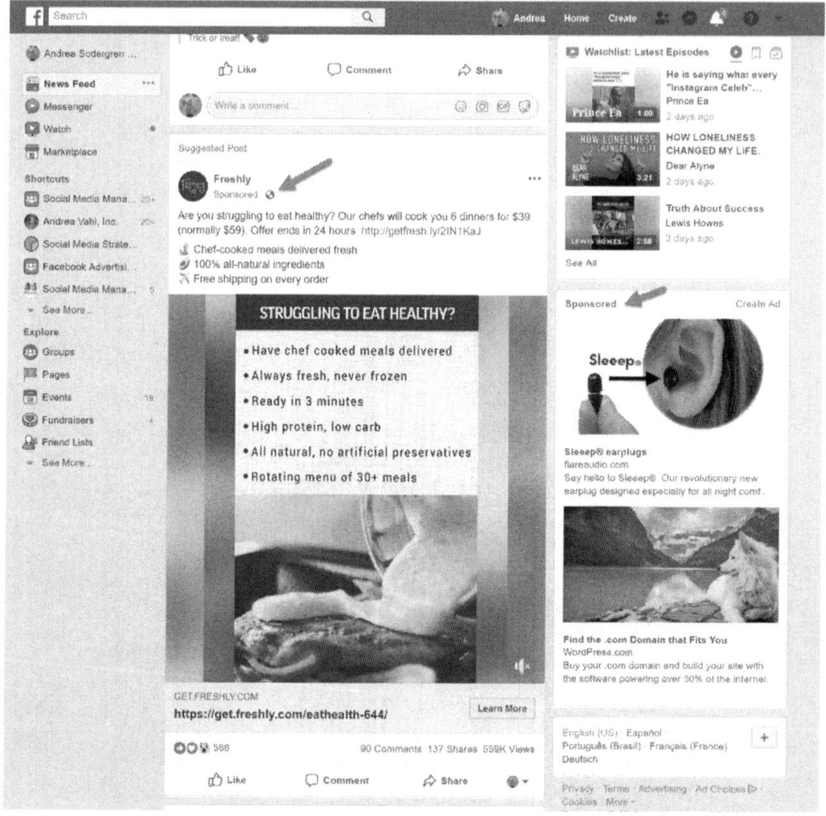

Facebook uses the demographic data you entered when you create an account with them to target ads toward you, as well as interests and Pages that you have liked. Facebook doesn't share exactly how they gather audiences for the target keywords you can use. So if we use a general term like "yoga," this may be a compilation of many Facebook Pages about yoga as well as the fact that someone has actually put into their Facebook Profile that they like yoga.

As I previously mentioned, you can also use something called "Audiences" - also known as "Custom Audiences" - to target people who have interacted with your Page, watched your videos, visited your website, subscribed to your email list, and more. This type of targeting needs a couple extra steps in order to create ads with Audiences.

Facebook ads are a little different from Google ads. With Google ads, you can target your ads to people based on their demographics, but you are also choosing search terms that someone is using right at that moment. If someone is searching with a search term "golf club reviews" or the best price on a certain type of golf club, then you might see that they are in a buying mode. But on Facebook, you could target someone who likes golf but they may have just purchased golf clubs last week. They aren't interested in buying more golf clubs. Or maybe they are because some golfers are a little crazy about clubs.

On Facebook, there's no way to target any search data. People aren't typically using the search function as much on Facebook anyway. People are scrolling through the news feed, possibly avoiding work (or is that just me? Oh wait, Facebook is my work). People might ask for references or recommendations in their posts, but we're not able to target those types of things.

With Facebook ads the most important thing is to catch someone's eye and get them to stop scrolling. I say all the time, the **goal is to Stop the Scroll!** The most critical parts of the ad are:

1. The targeting
2. The image or video
3. The text

We can argue about what order these elements are in all day long but this is the right order based on my almost 10 years of running Facebook ads for a wide variety of clients.

FACEBOOK AD OBJECTIVES AND FORMATS

Facebook has different types of Facebook Ad formats and different objectives you can choose for your Facebook Ads. The simplest type of ad is the "Boosted Post." A Boosted Post is typically done right from your Facebook Page and Facebook is often encouraging you as a Page owner to boost posts that are doing well. (Facebook will do anything to get business owners to spend money with them - hey, want to boost this post? How about now?). The Boosted Post is very easy to do because all you have to do is click the Boost Post button on any post on your Facebook Page.

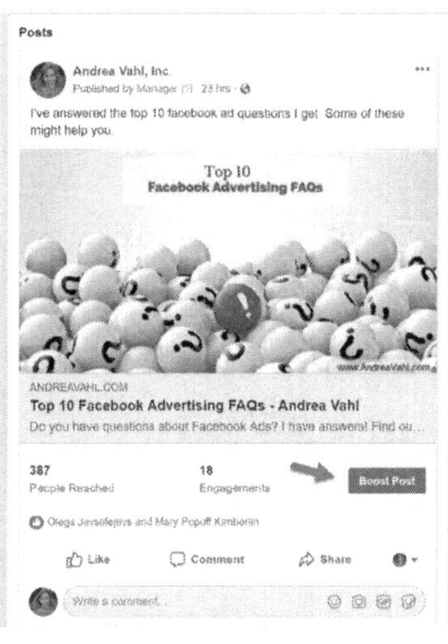

We'll talk more about Boosting Posts in the Starting Simple section. But a Boosted Post looks like any other ad in the News Feed. You do have some choices with budget and targeting when boosting a post, but running Facebook Ads from the Ads Manager offers more options for the refinement of your ad. Think of the Boosted Post as the candy bar that might satisfy a craving but not quite as effective as a healthy meal in terms of getting you the best results.

Facebook has a much wider spectrum of ads you can run in the Ads Manager platform which is typically connected to your Facebook profile (I know it seems a little counterintuitive that the Ads Manager is connected to your profile rather than your Page, but that's how it is). Your Ads Manager can also be part of what's called the Business Manager, which I will also touch on later in the book.

Ads can also be in different formats within each objective. Examples of different formats include:

- Single image ads
- Video ads
- Carousel ads (multiple images that you can scroll through)
- Slideshow video ads (still images that advance automatically)
- "Instant Experience" ads previously known as Canvas ads (available only on mobile devices and have both video and images)

Facebook will continue to add new types of ad formats and it often pays to be an early adopter in testing something new because it stands out from the other posts. Remember: the goal is to Stop the Scroll!

When you get into the Ads Manager and create an ad, you'll have lots of choices. This can feel overwhelming. Don't worry—remember this is Facebook Ads Made SIMPLE, not Facebook Ads Made Scary. I'll show you what the best choices are for most businesses.

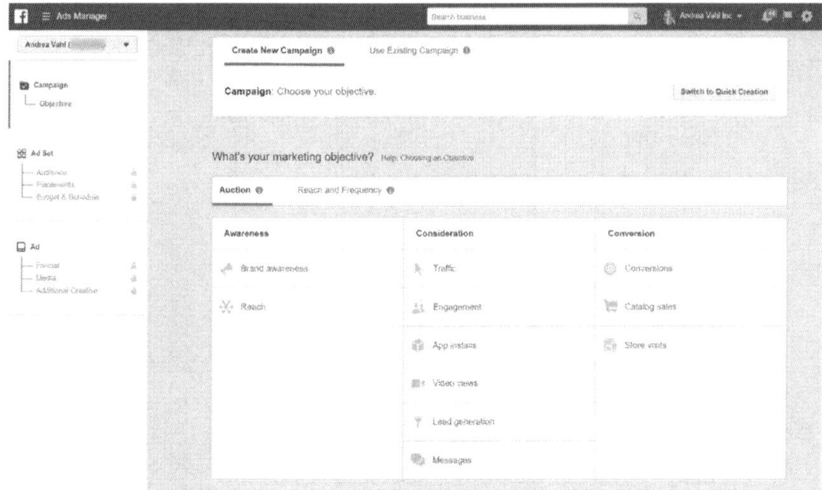

Your ad will be optimized for the marketing objective you choose. If you select that you want traffic, Facebook will show your ad to people who are likely to click on ads. If you select Lead generation, Facebook will show your ad to the people who like to fill out lead generation forms.

One of the most powerful Objectives you can choose is Conversions which can be good for generating leads and sales. But that objective does require a little more setup than just a Traffic ad. In this book, I show you how to run a Traffic ad and then set up a Conversion ad in Chapter 16 of the the Advanced Topics Section. We are going to start simple and then move to the more advanced methods—baby steps, so it's not too overwhelming!

Any marketing objective is still optimized within the targeting parameters you choose. So if you chose to show your ad to Parents in California between the ages of 25-35, that targeting would still be what is used. Facebook also optimizes the ad to the marketing objective you have. Remember that Facebook (and the whole internet for that matter) is tracking what we do so that they know the people who like to click on ads, watch videos, or buy products online.

HOW BIDDING WORKS

Facebook has two types of ways to bid: Auction or Reach and Frequency. Facebook ads are typically best optimized when they are using the Auction Bidding system (which is the default selection). Auction bidding means that you are competing against all the other people who are advertising on Facebook and using the same keywords or demographic targeting as you are.

The best ad placement will go to the highest bidder but other factors are in play, such as how well your ad is performing. Reach and Frequency is where you pay a fixed price to reach a certain amount of people (similar to a newspaper ad where you would have a fixed subscriber number). I will focus only on the Auction Bidding system in this book.

You can set your bid for how much you are willing to pay for a click or for 1000 people to see your ad (also known as CPM - cost per mille - which is French for 1000 - I don't know why we needed to bring the French into this whole thing, but for some reason we did).

You can also let Facebook do the optimization and have them give you the "lowest cost" bid. When I first heard that, I thought "Oh right, Facebook is going to do my bidding for me . That's like handing over your wallet and telling them to take what they want." But I have done my testing and this optimization strategy actually works well.

If you do set a bid amount, that is the highest you will ever pay for a click or 1000 impressions (CPM). Typically you won't often pay the full bid amount that you set; it's usually lower. But if you bid too low, your ad won't show because Facebook has other bidders that are willing to pay more for the ad space.

Your ad design and good targeting can help you get cheaper clicks. Facebook likes when good ads and interesting content are in the News Feed because that helps people enjoy Facebook more and keeps them surfing longer. Facebook will reward good ads with cheaper clicks and better results. So if your ad is a dud, you'll end up paying higher prices (but never higher than what you bid).

WHAT YOU CAN AND CAN'T ADVERTISE ON FACEBOOK

Before you do too far down the path of setting up Facebook ad campaigns, make sure your product or service complies with Facebook Ads policies. Familiarize yourself with how you can phrase your ads, and what you can and can't say. If you violate Facebook's policies, they will disapprove your ads and may even shut down your Facebook Ads account without warning. And their is often no explanation in the appeals process other than "you violated our policies." It's their sandbox and you have to play by their rules. The complete policies are here: https://www.facebook.com/policies/ads/

Here are some of the major prohibited items:

- Tobacco
- Illegal products
- Illegal or recreational drugs (sorry, legalized states - that's how it is)

- Unsafe supplements (this is determined by Facebook in its sole discretion)
- Weapons, ammunition, or explosives
- Adult products and adult content
- Surveillance equipment
- MLM - Multilevel Marketing companies

There are more prohibited items, but I've listed some of the major ones. Restricted items are moderated more heavily by Facebook (either by having you jump through some hoops to run the ad or check a box agreeing to their policies). These items include:

- Alcohol (some countries prohibit ads referencing alcohol and you must comply with local laws)
- Dating sites (require written permission)
- Gambling and state lotteries
- Online pharmacies and supplements
- Financial services and student loan services
- Politics or Issues of National Importance (require authorization)
- Cryptocurrency
- Drug and Alcohol Addiction Treatment Centers

Again, there are more heavily restricted items than are listed here. Make sure you familiarize yourself with the entire list.

Facebook's policies also cover how the ads appear or are written as well as the website that the ad might direct people to. Here are some of the major policies to be aware of when writing your ad or developing the web page that the ad goes to.

- Personal Attributes - the ad must not contain content that asserts or implies something personal. Such as "Are you overweight?" or "Do you have diabetes?"
- Before and After pictures
- Bad grammar or profanity - the ad needs to use good grammar and punctuation and not use any profanity.
- Sensational, controversial, misleading or false content
- Non-functional landing page on your website
- Nonexistent functionality - the most common issue is an image of a "play button" on an image so people try to click on it
- Facebook's brand assets cannot be in an image - you can't use the blue and white "f" logo or the full Facebook logo in your images

Facebook has an automated review process for ads and so occasionally a "non-compliant" ad will slip through but they often follow the review up with a more manual process. So if you see an ad that violates one of these policies, it usually isn't up for long. Facebook also does review the website that the ad goes to, so if the website is not within their policies they may disapprove the ad even if it is in compliance.

Typically, Facebook will just disapprove an ad that isn't following their policies. But sometimes Facebook will shut down the account. You can appeal an ad if you think it does comply, but it's much harder to restore a deactivated account. So just try to stay on Facebook's good side by following the policies in the first place. Grandma Mary says so.

3

UNDERSTANDING BASIC AD TERMS

Not only are you learning a new skill with Facebook Ads, but you are learning a new language! It can feel overwhelming. Sometimes people love to sprinkle this jargon into their sentences like Himalayan sea salt on top of a pretentious filet. Stay away from people who don't take the time to explain these terms to you. I've never been a fan of acronyms myself, but I do have to admit they can speed up conversations so I've been known to toss a few about.

This book covers these terms in more depth than the different sections, so don't feel you have to memorize everything right now (seriously there is no test at the end of this book). But you can bookmark this chapter and come back to it if you need it.

Facebook actually does a decent job of giving you definitions in the places you might need them. But all too often, Facebook has a bit of an agenda when making recommendations on what works best. All you need to do when you see a word you aren't familiar with is mouse over the word—often a popup box will appear with the definition. When there is a "See More" link in the popup box, you can click on that and get even MORE information.

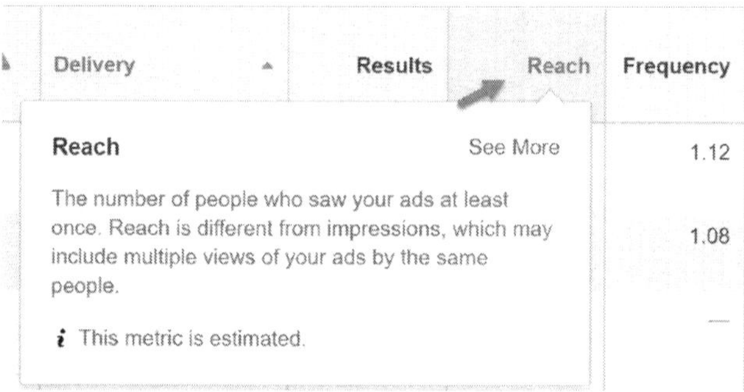

I get it, the definition doesn't always help. But at least it's there! The terms will start to make sense eventually as you learn this new language, so be gentle with yourself.

GENERAL FACEBOOK TERMS AND FREQUENTLY USED AD TERMS

Facebook Algorithm: If you saw every single potential piece of content in your News Feed, you would be overwhelmed and you would miss news that's important to you (that's more how Twitter works - oooh, sorry Twitter fans). So Facebook limits what you see and shows you more of the things they think you would be interested in. They keep track of who you interact with most and which pieces of content are interesting to the most people, then typically show you the most recent pieces of content that meet both standards. Facebook puts more emphasis on personal connections and your Groups than posts by Pages.

Funnel or Marketing Funnel: Many people use this term to refer to the steps it takes to bring someone from a potential client to a sale. For example someone might see an ad on Facebook, opt in to get a coupon from you, get an email from you, and then buy your product.

Email List: Your business email list should use a software system like Constant Contact, Mailchimp, Aweber, or other service that may also be connected to your "shopping cart" where people can make purchases online from you. Even if you don't have an online store, I do suggest you sign up for some service so that you can build your email list with potential buyers that you communicate with. Facebook could go away tomorrow and you want to have something that you "own" so that you can connect with your potential customers.

Landing Page: A landing page is just a website page typically optimized for ad traffic so that people take a specific action like make a purchase or sign up for your email list. Usually you want a landing page to be free from lots of other distractions like things in a side bar or a big menu.

Lead Magnet: Optin Monster (a tool used to get email signups) defines a Lead Magnet very well: "A lead magnet is an incentive that marketers offer to potential buyers in exchange for their email address, or other contact information. Lead magnets usually offer a piece of digital, downloadable content, such as a free PDF checklist, report, eBook, whitepaper, video, etc." Your Lead Magnet could also be a coupon or a 15 minute free consultation. Think about what your audience would really value from you. The best Lead Magnets could be something you would potentially sell but you actually give away - hard to think about. But believe me, you'll benefit in the end when you are able to grow your email list easily.

Key Performance Indicator or KPI: A metric that you use to show exactly what is most important. For example if you were a basketball player who wanted to get better at shooting baskets, the KPI might be how many baskets you made out of how many you shot. If you wanted to get faster, you would measure how fast you ran across the court. The metric can change depending on your real goal. And you have to make sure you know what that metric is and know how to measure it so you can compare each ad against each other. As Peter Drucker said, "You can't manage what you can't measure."

News Feed: The section in the center column of your Home when you log into Facebook. Posts from your friends, Groups you are in, Pages you Like, and Ads all appear here. The News Feed is unique to you based on who you are connected to, so don't worry if you see posts from your crazy nephew - no one else you are friends with will see those posts unless they are also friends with your crazy nephew. Unless you interact with that post—so be careful.

Opt In: I use this term often to describe the act of someone requesting something that you are giving away (a Lead Magnet) in exchange for some of their information like an email address or phone number. You want someone to freely give their information to you in exchange for something that they would value (a coupon, an ebook, a video training, a white paper, a free consultation, a webinar, etc.). Then you can follow up with people and hopefully turn that exchange into a sale of your product or service at some point. To see an example of a landing page where someone would "opt in" to my email list and get a freebie, go to https://fbadvertisingsecrets.com/freecourse.

Here is an example of an Optin form where I give away an ebook:

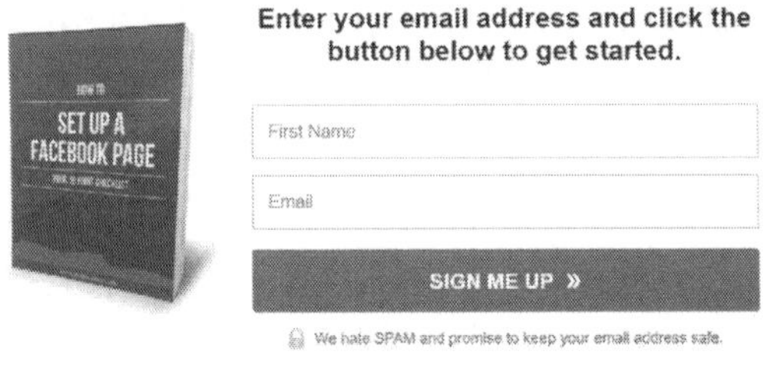

Power Editor: You may hear this term, but the Power Editor tool is no longer available in Facebook. All the functionality that was in Power Editor is now in the regular Ads Manager.

Retargeting: Retargeting is essentially just how it sounds - targeting someone again. So if someone has been to your website, liked your Facebook Page, or watched one of your videos, you can "retarget" them with an ad. This is your warm audience, because they have already had some experience with you and might be more receptive to your ad.

ROI - Return on Investment: A common marketing term that essentially compares how much you invested with how much you made. ROI is typically expressed as a ratio or a percentage but can just mean that it's important to make sure you are getting something back for your investment. No one wants to keep dumping into a black hole of bad Facebook ads.

Split Test: A method of testing that keeps all factors consistent except for 1 change (ideally) so that when you look at the results you know the difference in results was due to that single change. The term split test can have slightly different meanings but the idea is to have a method of testing to keep improving your results.

TYPES OF FACEBOOK ADS

Boost Post: This ad is created right from your Facebook Page. The purpose of this type of post is to "push" it into the News Feed of either your Fans and their friends or people you choose through targeting. The goal of this post is usually to get engagement on the post itself but sometimes can be optimized for traffic to your website or video views.

Brand Awareness: This ad is optimized for "Brand Awareness" and typically has better reach than other ads but doesn't drive traffic to a website very well.

Reach: This ad is optimized for Reach and gets shown to the most people for the cheapest cost but also doesn't often drive traffic to a website at a good cost.

Traffic: Use this type of ad for sending traffic to any website.

Engagement: Within the Engagement ad, you can select that you want to get more Post Responses (like the Boost Post except created in Ads Manager), Page Likes, or Event Responses (Facebook Events only).

App Installs: If you have created a Facebook App (like a game or some stand-alone program) you can advertise the App with this ad.

Video Views: Use this ad ONLY when you want cheaper video views. If you really want to drive traffic or get conversions but want to have video in the ad, you should use a Traffic or Conversion ad and just use video in the ad itself.

Lead Generation: A Lead Generation ad is an ad that doesn't require a website. The lead capture form is contained on Facebook and the person never has to leave Facebook. The lead form will be "prefilled" with the person's contact information that is a part of their Facebook profile so that it's very easy to "opt in."

Messages: Use this type of ad to drive traffic to your Facebook Page Messenger to have a 1:1 conversation with you.

Conversions: This is the best type of ad to measure your Return on Investment. Use it with a Conversion Pixel to track sales, e-mail optins, and other actions that people can take on your website. You need a place to put the conversion pixel on your website that indicates the visitor has been through the desired action such as a "thank you" page.

Catalog Sales: ONLY for businesses who have created an online Catalog through the Business Manager. Best for e-commerce companies with a large number of items.

Store Visits: ONLY for businesses that have MULTIPLE Facebook locations on one Facebook Page (think Starbucks or Home Depot).

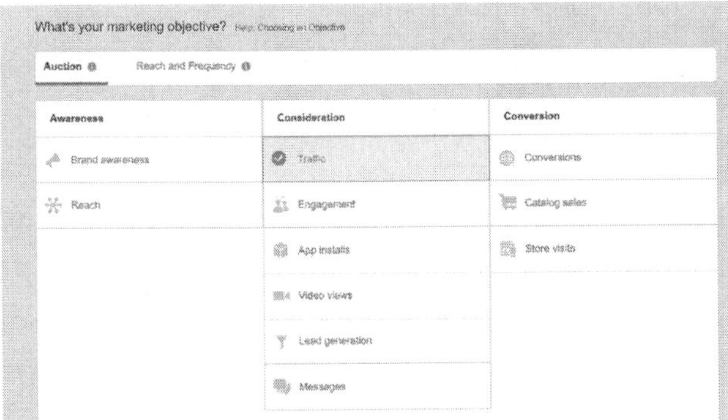

You might be thinking, "Yikes there are a LOT of choices here. How do I pick the right objective?" Or you might be thinking,

"Forget all these terms, I'll just skip ahead and let Andrea tell me what to do." That is absolutely fine! The good news is that only a few of these Objectives are right for beginners and I'll tell you all about the best selections in Chapter 13. So you don't have to worry as much about all the other choices.

FACEBOOK AD TERMS USED DURING THE AD CREATION PROCESS

Ad: The actual "creative" section where you set your image or video, your text, the link you are using if you are trying to drive traffic. What the ad looks like.

Ad Set: In this section you choose the demographics and keywords you use, the placements (where the ad appears), the budget, and the schedule for your ads. Any ads that are IN this ad set all use the same settings that you choose at this level.

Campaign: Many people use this term more generally to talk about Ad Campaigns, but in the Facebook Ads Manager, the structure is set up as Campaign (the overall Objective), Ad Set (the targeting and budgeting area), and Ad (the image and text of the ad). Multiple Ad Sets and Ads can be "under" one Campaign.

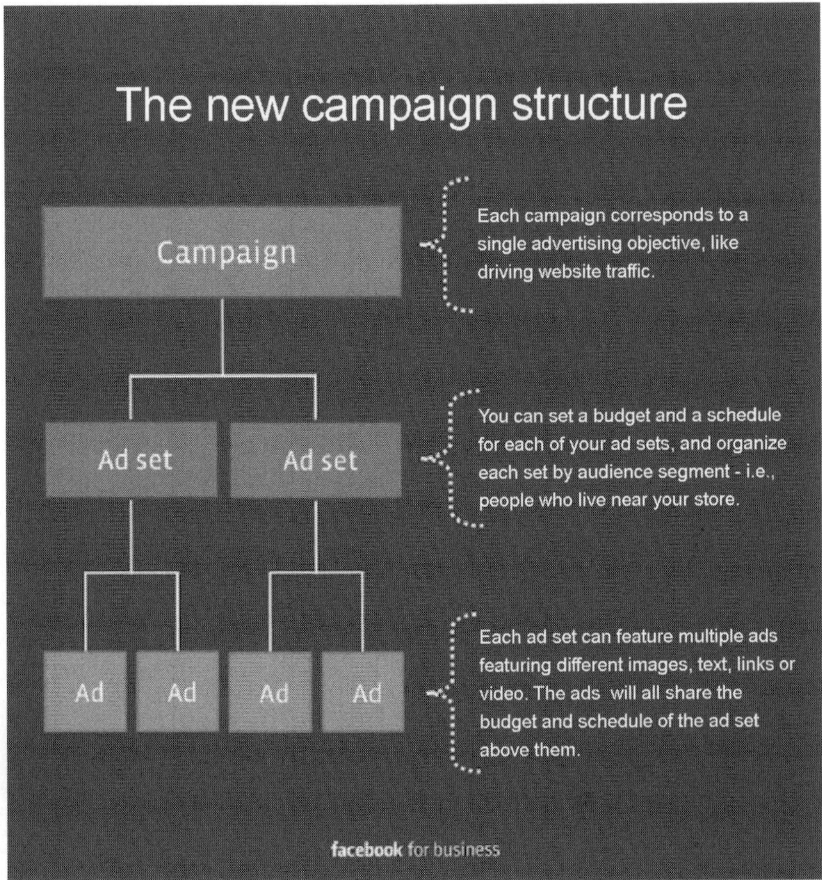

Carousel: This is a type of ad that has multiple images that you swipe through (more on this in Chapter 10: Creating Your Ad Image).

Connections: Include or exclude your current fans, or friends of fans in your targeting. You can only use the Pages you are an admin of in this section. Only use this setting if you want to limit your Ad to just that targeting.

CTA: Call to Action. The typical meaning for this in the Facebook ad is the "Call to Action button" that can be on the ad that says

"Learn More" or "Shop Now" or many other preset phrases. But, in general, this can also mean a specific next step that you ask the person to take in the ad or on your website like "Call us now to find out more".

Custom Audiences: Groups of people you set up in the "Audiences" section of Facebook like your website visitors, people who have watched your videos, people who are on your email list, and more.

Detailed Targeting: Use keywords to target your Ad. The keywords are based on the Pages people have liked, TV shows they have watched, or other things they have added to their profile. Keep in mind that not all keywords are available, and not all people actually put their interests in their profile. You can also put other Page names in this section to target the Fans of those Pages.

Facebook Pixel: A bit of code that you place in the header, footer, or somewhere on a web page that will track if someone comes from a Facebook ad and lands on that web page. Typically installed on a web page at the end of a sequence of events that happen on your website that indicates someone has completed the desired action.

Offer: A Facebook Offer is a special type of ad that people "claim" and then typically get a discount. It's a unique type of ad that Facebook puts into the ad creation process but isn't something you should try first if you are a beginner.

Placements and Automatic Placements: You can choose where your ad shows up on all the available places Facebook has to advertise. I recommend to NEVER choose Automatic Placements because you want to choose exactly where your ad appears. Some placement choices include: Facebook Feeds, Right Column, Marketplace, Instagram, Audience Network, and Messenger.

FACEBOOK AD TERMS IN THE REPORTS

The Facebook Reporting section has a LOT of terms and columns you can see so I won't go into every single term. This list shows the most common terms you should know.

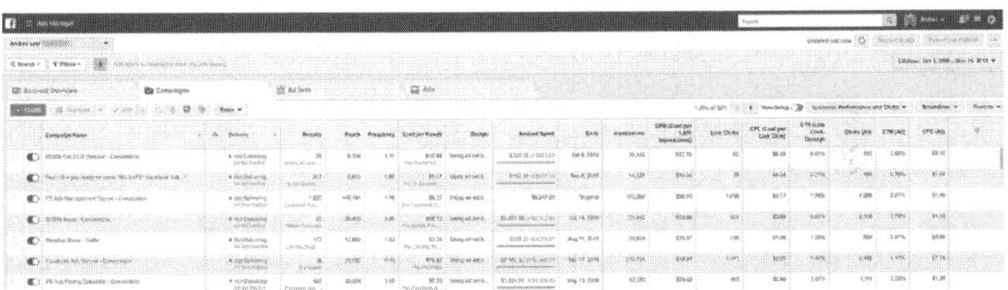

Clicks: The actual number of clicks of the ad. This report can include a click if someone liked your fan Page right from the ad itself. A single user could click on your ad multiple times. Clicks can be anywhere in the ad (the photo, the link, etc.)

Cost per Result: You can see exactly how much it cost per Landing Page View, Conversion, Page Like etc - whichever Objective you set up at the "Campaign" level. You can't compare these results against each other - make sure you are comparing like metrics to really understand how the ads performed.

CPC (cost per click): How much each click your ad received actually cost you. This number is calculated even if you didn't bid on the CPC model, which is helpful for comparison. It takes how many clicks your ad received (even if you're paying by impression) and calculates how much each click cost you.

CPM (cost per thousand impressions): How much each 1000 impressions cost. Even if you didn't bid with the CPM model when you placed your ad, Facebook Reports will calculate it for your reference.

CTR: Click Through Rate. How many times your ad was clicked, divided by the number of times your ad was shown (impressions). This is a straight ratio of the Clicks divided by Impressions.

Delivery: In the Delivery column in the Report section, you can tell if the ad is currently delivering or has finished and if it isn't running, you will see why the ad isn't running (i.e. the ad wasn't approved, the ad is turned off at the Ad level, or it's complete).

Filter: You can Filter your view to show different types of ads or ads that have certain variables in common like age ranges, objectives, or placements.

Frequency: The average number of times each person saw your ad. This is the Impressions divided by the Reach.

Impressions: How many times the ad has been shown to a Facebook user. Ads can be shown multiple times to users if they are logging in several times during your campaign, or if they are browsing through different areas of Facebook.

Landing Page Views: This metric is available if you have the Facebook Pixel installed on your site and is a measure of how many people came from your ad and then waited for your website to load (as opposed to just clicking on the link and hitting the back button before seeing your site).

Link Clicks: Only the clicks on the actual link that is in the ad. I watch this statistic very closely in addition to Landing Page Views because you typically are trying to drive actual traffic to your website.

Reach: The number of people who saw your ads. The reach is different from the Impressions because it only counts the unique people who have seen your ad.

Spend: The amount you spent for the time summary you chose for the report.

ADVANCED FACEBOOK AD TERMS

Canvas Ad: An advanced ad layout that includes videos, carousel ads, and text that you can design. The ad operates only on mobile and provides an interactive experience.

Dynamic Creative: You can have Facebook change the ads headline, images, text and more automatically based on how they see it performing. As a beginner, I think it's best to set up your own testing initially so you don't have to worry about this feature to start.

Lookalike Audiences: (a.k.a. Similar Audience) Start with the Custom Audience, and then create a new, larger list of Facebook users who have similar interests to your list.

As we progress through the chapters, I will go deeper into the meaning and significance of these terms . This is just your sample to get you started. A buzzword appetizer if you will. Hope you enjoyed it!

4

SETTING UP YOUR FACEBOOK ADS STRATEGY

Do you have a clear Facebook Ads strategy? Many people just kind of wing it when it comes to their Facebook Ads. That's why you are so much smarter by getting your strategy in place first! Look at you with your big brain!

Sometimes it's hard to really know what your strategy should be because you may not know everything that Facebook Ads can do for you. The other challenge is knowing what to expect in terms of results. You'll learn more about that in the Typical Results chapter.

If you don't have a strategy with specific goals in place for your Facebook Ads, you won't know if you're getting a return on your efforts! Your Facebook marketing strategy shouldn't live in a vacuum – it needs to be integrated with your overall marketing plan.

BEFORE YOU START

Before you start marketing on Facebook, you should have these things in place:

1. A good website and/or landing page. Your website is the hub of your business and should look professional and showcase what you have to offer your customers. The place where you send your Facebook ad traffic to has to clearly show the benefits of your product or service.
2. A clear business model and plan. How are you making money? This sounds obvious, but many entrepreneurs don't have a solid business plan and don't understand things like the cost of goods or how much money they can (and should) allocate towards marketing. If you are just starting out, you can use Facebook to gain awareness but use one of the ad types that will benefit you most (find out more in the next chapter).
3. An email marketing delivery service. Some large consumer products may not need an email delivery system but most businesses still need to use email marketing as part of their overall marketing strategy. email is not dead and is your best chance of being seen by the bulk of your current and potential customers. There are many email providers out there to choose from including ConstantContact, Aweber, InfusionSoft, MailChimp, and more. Find one that fits with your needs and budget.
4. An optimized Facebook Page. Before you start marketing on Facebook, get the basic elements of a good Facebook Page in place. Your Page doesn't have to have a lot of Fans

in order to run Ads (it can even be a brand new Page). But you do need to have things like a cover photo, a profile photo, and I would also say an optimized About section where you talk about your business.

There can be exceptions to these "requirements," such as if you're advertising for brand awareness and not trying to send people to a website, or using Lead Generation ads so that you don't have to send people to your website. But in general, this is darn good list to start with.

You also may need a "lead magnet" as covered in the last chapter. But the lead magnet doesn't have to be hard to create.

STEPS TO DEVELOP YOUR ADS STRATEGY

Once you have the basic elements in place, you can begin to integrate your Facebook ads with your overall marketing plan. Here are 4 steps to get your Facebook Ads strategy in place:

#1: SET GOALS

Any strategy begins with goals. What do you want out of your Facebook Ads? Sales is the obvious choice but there can also be secondary goals that lead to sales.

Consider some of these Facebook marketing goals as you craft your plan:

- **Increasing overall exposure and awareness.** The measurement of this goal could come in the form of new Likes to your Page, video views, or traffic to your website.

Attach a specific and attainable figure to this goal (i.e. 500 new website visitors in the next 3 months).

- **Creating a loyal, engaged community.** You may be doing this by just boosting your posts to your "warm" audience or you may be sending Facebook Ad traffic to a Facebook Group to grow that. In order for people to do business with you, they usually want to get to know, like, and trust you first. Creating an engaged community can help facilitate that trust.
- **Establish authority and showcase your knowledge.** Facebook is a perfect place to showcase your past work, in-depth knowledge of your subject matter, and your personality in terms of how your company works.

- **Gather leads.** Using Facebook as a lead generator is a great strategy. Using some type of email optin is a great way to gather information from people who may be interested in your product or service. You can give away a freebie that relates to your product, host a free webinar that may have an offer at the end, or run a contest that gives away your product to the winner. Some companies have a free trial of their product available to their Facebook audience. Or even if it isn't completely free, an offering like that can be

a good way to give people a flavor of your product or service.

- **Attendees for your event.** This goal may overlap with sales if your event is paid, but you could also be trying to get attendees at a free event (like an art show, open house, or business expo). If you set up your event through Facebook, you can advertise that event or advertise online registration on your website or a tool like Eventbrite.
- **Foot traffic to your location.** This is one of the hardest goals to measure unless you ask every single person entering your store how they heard about you (even then, they may forget). One way to measure is to have a special coupon code just for people who saw your Facebook Ad or use a tool called "Offline Events" in Facebook Ads. This tool requires that you get either an email or a phone number with every checkout, so it isn't a perfect system.
- **Sales.** Selling directly from Facebook to a "cold" audience can be a challenge. If the checkout occurs on your website, you can use the Facebook Pixel to track your sales. Often, people need a special limited deal in order to purchase. The limits could be time (you only offer the product during certain periods),price, or quantity. Early bird specials can also motivate people to purchase.
- **New donors for your non-profit.** This goal is very similar to sales if people can donate on your website and you have the pixel installed. You can go on to track the donations as a result of each ad type.

There are a lot of options and your business model may be complicated. You may want to map out the customer journey as to how someone comes to do business with you and give you money.

For example, a blogger may be looking for bigger awareness with potential advertisers or sponsors. So they decide to run a video ad to get a lot of visible engagement with their blog. The point is that you know better than anyone what types of activities drive the progression to money for your business.

As I mentioned, Facebook doesn't always work well for straight sales. You can target people based on their interests and demographics, but you can't target people based on the fact that they are searching for your product right now like with Google Ads.

So sometimes, it's better to lead people who are on Facebook to a step that happens before they buy. Warm them up a little with your information and content before asking for the sale. People need a little romancing!

You may have different goals for different parts of your sales cycle. One thing that I know in my business is that when I get more email subscribers, I get more sales later. They don't always buy something right away. But I can connect with them through good content and they buy 6 months or a year later.

#2: SET UP YOUR TRACKING METHODS

The biggest part of your success is being able to measure it so that you know what's working. When you set up an ad with a particular objective, Facebook can easily track that objective.

If you want leads or sales, you can measure sales directly from Facebook ads if the lead or sale happens on your website with the help of the Facebook Pixel. But you will have to take an extra step in setting up the tracking with either a Custom

Conversion or a Standard Event Code (see the chapter on Facebook Pixel and the Advanced Topics section for more information).

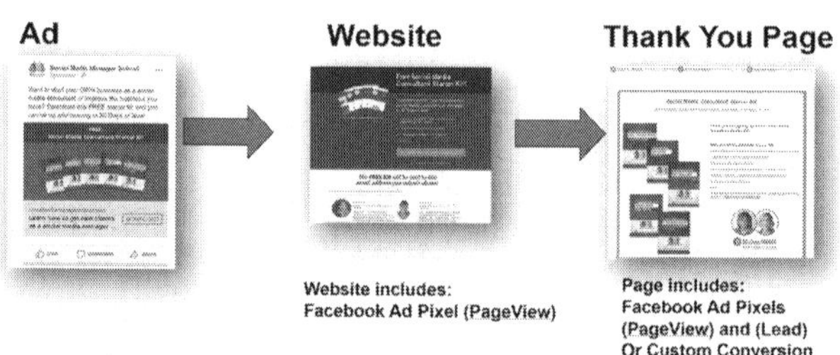

If the sale happens offline (either at your location or with someone calling you for example), then you will have to determine how you will track that. You could ask people if they saw your ad but that doesn't always work.

If the sale for your product happens on another website like Amazon, then that is not easy to track. You typically can't install the Facebook tracking Pixel on other websites. You may use Google Analytics to help track what happens to the traffic that comes from Facebook after it lands on your site.

#3: MATCH YOUR GOAL TO A KEY PERFORMANCE INDICATOR AND AD OBJECTIVE

In order to measure your success and compare which ads are working best for you, you need to choose a Key Performance Indicator - also known as KPI.

Some business objectives could have several possible key performance indicators depending on your assets, what type of ad you were running, and your strategy.

Here are some possible examples of a business objective matched to a Key Performance Indicator in Facebook Ads:

BUSINESS OBJECTIVE

Key Performance Indicator

- Engagement
- Cost per Engagement on post
- Traffic to website
- Cost per link click or landing page view (if the Pixel is installed)
- Reaching new potential customers
- Cost per Lead/Conversion
- Cost per Video View (brand awareness)
- Cost per link click or landing page view
- Cost per 1000 Impressions (CPM) (brand awareness)
- Cost per Message on Facebook (Messenger Ad)
- Sales
- Cost per Purchase (as measured by the Pixel)
- Establishing expertise or authority
- Cost per 1000 Impressions (CPM) (brand awareness)
- Cost per link click or landing page view
- Cost per Lead/Conversion

Next, you'll take the Business Objective you have and determine what type of ad you will run. I think most businesses should focus on a Traffic or Conversion ad, or possibly Lead Generation.

But if you are looking for Brand Awareness and the highest reach you can get (and don't necessarily care about traffic to your website), a Reach objective or Brand Awareness objective may be a better fit.

#4: CREATE A FACEBOOK AD CAMPAIGN PLAN AND SPLIT TEST YOUR FACEBOOK ADS

The next step in your Facebook Ad strategy is to develop a campaign plan where you will test different keywords, different images and different text in the ads.

Split Testing Ads – Group your Keywords

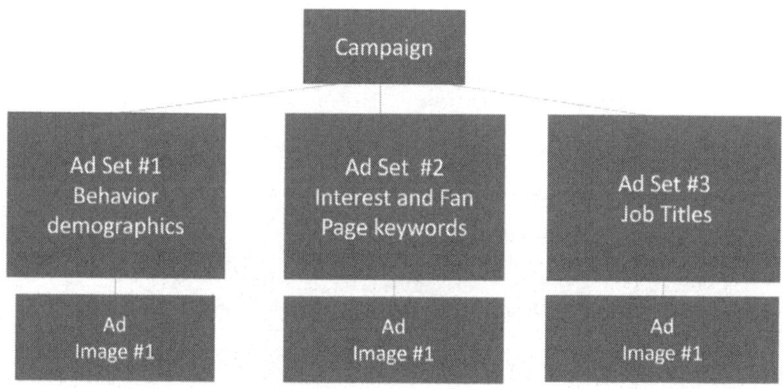

If your budget is small, you may only be able to test a couple different variations. But by testing at least two different things, you will have more information on what works better and be able to save money! I cover more on Split Testing in chapter 15.

To get started quickly, you can just choose one image and some demographics then circle back to testing a different variation later.

#5: MEASURE AND TWEAK YOUR FACEBOOK ADS

Your next step is to watch your key performance indicator and turn off the ads that aren't performing as well. So for example, if you are driving traffic and optimizing around link clicks, then you watch the ads that give you the best link click cost.

If you are optimizing around conversions, you will be able to easily see which image is performing better in your Ad reports and turn off the one that isn't converting as well.

For example, in this image, one of the ads is converting at $4.69 per conversion and the other is converting at $23.56 per conversion - over 5 TIMES as expensive! That is crazy! And really ridiculous, because I thought we looked really cute in that picture.

But it didn't convert. It's ok, I'm trying not to take it personally! Sniff.

Ad Name	Delivery	Results	Reach	Frequer	Cost per Result	Amount Spent	Ends	Relevan Scc
Jump Start 2018 - Conversions - ...	Not Delivering Ad Set is Off	262 Jump Start 2...	32,784	1.20	$4.69 Per Jump Sta...	$1,229.34	Jan 25, 2018	6
Jump Start 2018 - Conversions - ...	Not Delivering Ad Set is Off	8 Jump Start 2...	4,814	1.02	$23.56 Per Jump Sta...	$188.51	Jan 25, 2018	4
Results from 2 ads		270 Jump Start 2...	37,108 People	1.19 Per Person	$5.25 Per Jump Sta...	$1,417.85 Total Spent		

Remember: Facebook Advertising is not always going to give you an immediate return on your investment. But you will see long term benefits when you choose the best types of ads and create a testing plan.

Some people that purchase my products today have been on my email list for years. Different niches can have longer sales cycles. Marketing is a marathon, not a sprint. But we do have to make smart choices in how we are spending our money on Facebook.

STRATEGIES FOR BEGINNERS, INTERMEDIATE USERS, AND ADVANCED USERS

Your strategy will change as you get better at Facebook Ads and as your budget grows.

As a beginner, you may just focus on testing basic audiences and driving traffic to your website. Watch to see how the traffic converts or meets your objective. Your main focus will likely be growing your brand and using boosted posts to get your content in front of your audience.

An intermediate strategy is to create a lead magnet and grow your list with targeted ads. Run multiple split-test campaigns to determine your best audiences, your best images, experiment with different creative elements like videos or carousel ads. You might also do custom audiences for your targeting so that you can retarget your ads to your "warm" audience.

An advanced strategy could be to warm up the audience with different pieces of content, retarget traffic with ads for people who got to the Add To Cart page on your website but didn't complete the purchase, focusing on getting them from first touch to sale.

Facebook ads offer a lot of possibilities, but they aren't only good for advanced users. Beginners and intermediate users can also have success if you choose the right tactics and make smart choices on the types of ads you run.

5

THE FACEBOOK CAMPAIGN STRUCTURE

When you first create a Facebook ad, the interface might feel confusing and a little scary. But if you understand the Facebook Ad Campaign structure, you can navigate better and understand how to make the right choices at each level. Knowing the campaign structure is critical for split testing and understanding the Facebook ad reports.

The campaign structure is a hierarchy of Campaign, Ad Set, Ad.

At the Campaign level, you choose the objective like Traffic, Video Views, Conversions, etc.

The Ad Set level contains the targeting, placement, bidding, budget and schedule. You can have multiple Ad Sets underneath each Campaign or just one Ad Set.

At the Ad level, you create what the ad looks like. You have the image or video, the text of the ad, Call to Action button, and you also put the link there if you are sending traffic to a a website.

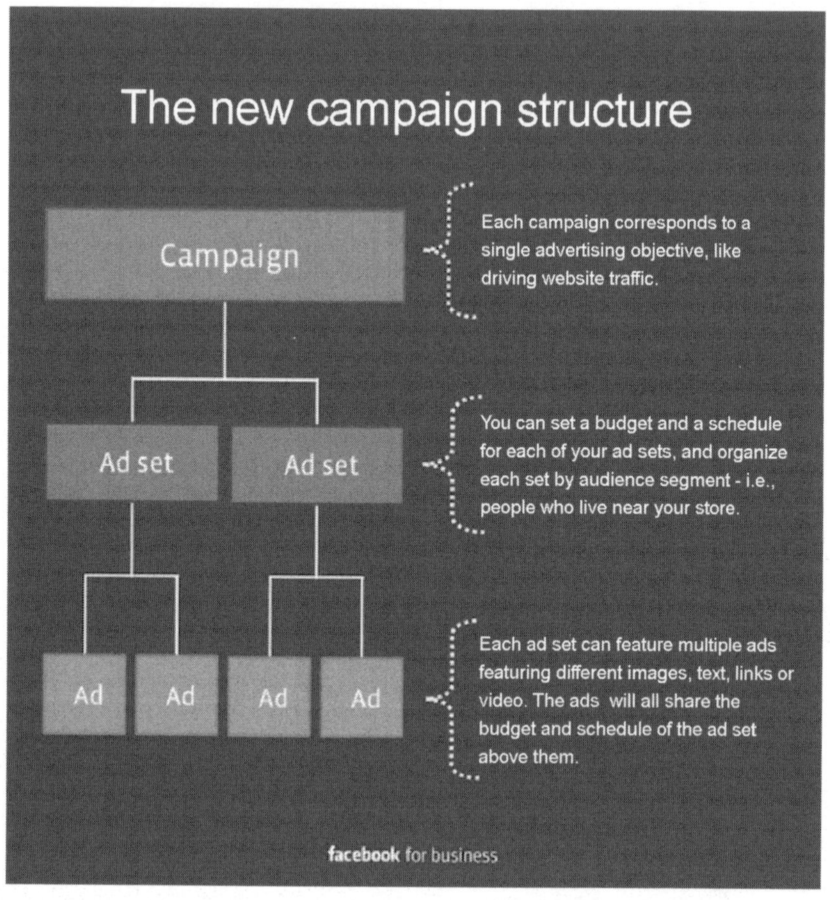

When you look at the flow of the ad campaign process, you see each of the levels (Campaign, Ad Set, Ad) on the left sidebar and you can navigate between the levels to make adjustments.

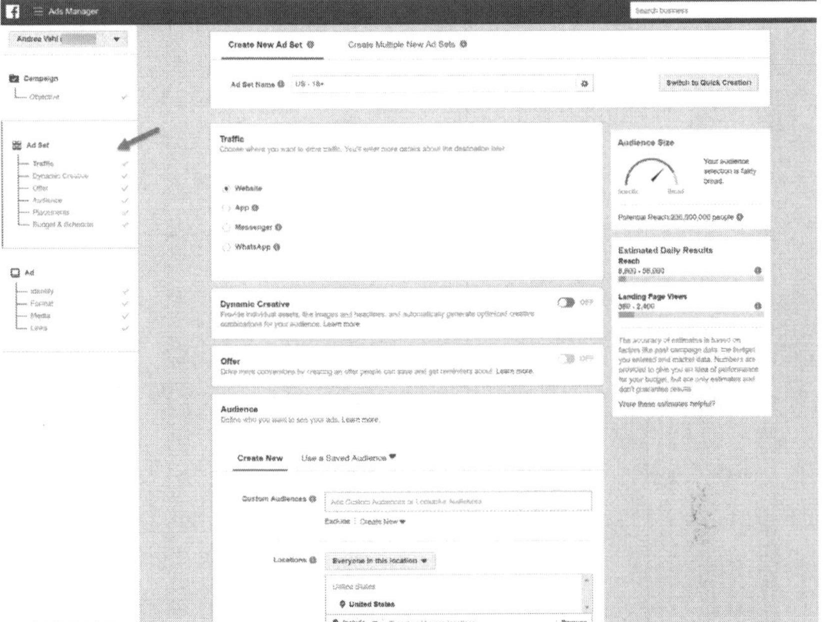

When you start running more ads, you can group all the same types of ads with the same objective under a single Campaign so that your Reports section is clearer. You should also have clear names for your Campaigns, Ad Sets and Ads. You can see in the image that the Ad Set name defaults to some basic information about the audience (in this case,US-18+), which isn't very descriptive.

When you have descriptive Ad and Ad Set names you can look at the reports and know a little bit about which ad you ran and easily see which one had the best results. I'll give you my general naming conventions in just a bit.

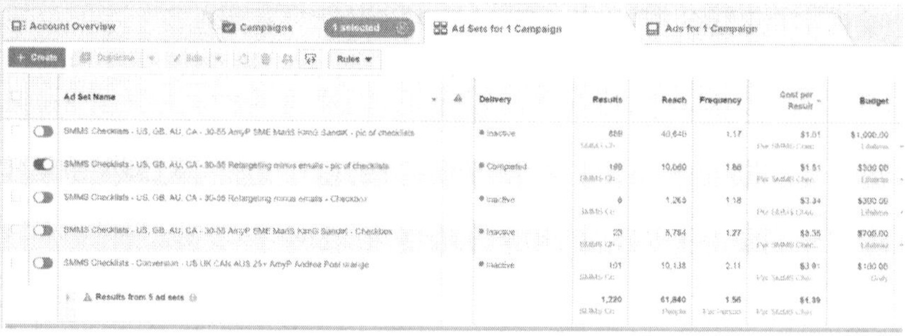

HOW TO GROUP YOUR CAMPAIGNS, AD SETS, AND ADS

Initially you will have one Campaign with one Ad Set and one Ad. Easy peasy. But then when you start adding more tests it can get confusing.

So if you are doing split testing with your ads, and you are changing a variety of things, then you may need to set up multiple Ad sets as well as multiple Campaigns.

Here are some examples of when you need a new Campaign, new Ad Set, or just a new Ad for different aspects you might split test.

Split testing that requires a new Campaign:

- Different types of ad objectives (i.e. Traffic vs. Conversion)
- Different website landing pages (actually, not totally necessary but a good idea)

Split testing that requires a new Ad set:

- Different targeting - you have one ad running to one set of keywords and demographics and another going to a different target

- Different bidding models - you may want to test a Facebook optimized bidding method and then one where you set the exact cost per click you want to pay
- Different placements - maybe you want to run one ad on mobile only and one ad on desktop, or you want to split out Instagram placement
- Ads that you want to run on a particular individual schedule automatically (i.e. one ad runs on Sunday and one ad runs on Monday – to turn these on automatically, they both need their own Ad set)
- Ads that you want to have a particular budget set for them individually without having Facebook decide which ad to give the budget to (you will create the Ad and have just one ad under each Ad Set, not multiple ads with multiple images)

Split testing that only requires new Ads:

- Different image or video
- Different copy
- Different call to action buttons

In the previous chapter, I showed an example of how I typically run tests—with one ad underneath each Ad Set. In this example, you have multiple ads under one Ad Set and that means that they all share the budget and the targeting and the schedule that you have at the Ad Set level. Facebook will "optimize" all the ads under the Ad Set and decide which one is performing the best and give more of the budget to that ad. This strategy can be good and bad because sometime Facebook doesn't decide correctly. Or it can decide too quickly which ad is performing the best and doesn't fully test the other ads.

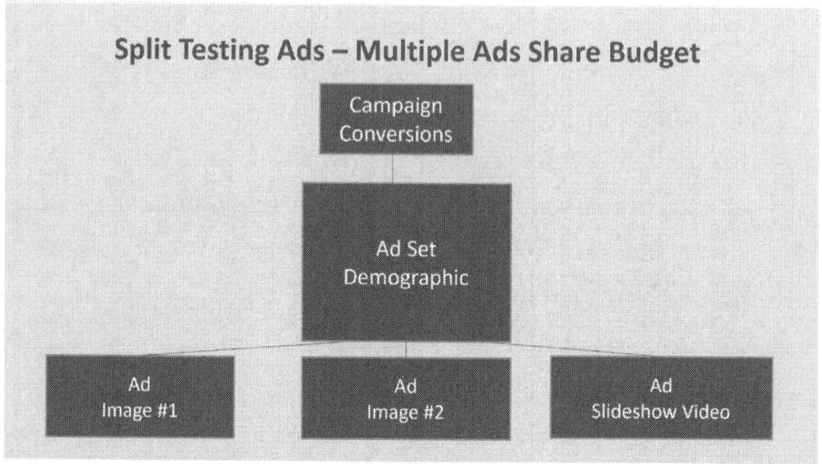

You will learn more about split testing in the Taking Action section of this book.

NAMING CONVENTIONS FOR CAMPAIGN, AD SETS, AND ADS

When you first start, you might be so excited about getting your first ad placed that you don't care what they are named. But the sooner you get in the habit of naming the levels well, the easier it will be in the future. Who wants to go back in and edit all their names later? Nopity nope nope!

Everyone has different ideas about how to name their campaigns and I've seen some marketers use a string of abbreviations to make them short while others have code words. The names really only have to make sense to you and your team so you get to decide! I'm going to share my naming conventions as an example.

Campaign Names

I keep my Campaign names short since that is the top of the "funnel" so to speak. Then you will drill down and get more specific at each level.

My naming convention for Campaigns is:

[Goal of the campaign or what I'm advertising] – [Objective set in Facebook]

So for example:

- Facebook Changes Webinar Feb 2016 – Conversions
- SMMS Sales Page - Traffic
- Book a call - Lead Generation

Each of these gives me an idea about where the traffic is going and what the objective is for that campaign. Then beneath that level, I can get more specific for each Ad Set and Ad.

Ad Set Names

At the Ad Set level, you are adding things like targeting and placement to the mix. You want to be able to look at your report and know what was different or unique about each different Ad Set. You don't want your names to be TOO long, but have just enough information so that you know what was unique.

I tend to keep my Campaign information in the title but you may choose not to. And if I'm testing just one ad underneath each Ad Set, I might put information about that ad in the Ad Set level.

My naming convention for Ad Sets is:

[Goal of the campaign] - [Objective] – [Demographics] - [Placement - if unique]

or

[Goal of the campaign] - [Objective] – [Demographics] - [Placement - if unique] – [Ad features - if just one ad]

So for example:

- Commuter Incentive Coupon - Traffic - Local Area 18-35 Environmental Interests - mobile only - Image w/o logo
- SMMS Checklists - Conversion - US UK CAN AUS 25+ Social Media Examiner - orange image

I may shorten some of these names if I know what the abbreviations mean.

Ad Names

If there is only one ad underneath each Ad Set, then I can just use the same name for both levels. The important thing is to be able to read the report and not have to open up the Ads or Ad Sets every time to see which was which.

If you have multiple ads underneath the Ad Set, then you can just add any features to the name.

[Goal of the campaign] - [Objective] – [Demographics] - [Placement - if unique] – [Ad features]You might be wondering why we are going through all of this background information before we get to the actual ad creation. But you will thank me later when you set up your ads the right way from the beginning!

Feel free to thank me on my Facebook Page at www.facebook.com/AndreaVahlinc/.

Or you can Like me. Please Like me. Haha. I also do take questions there if you need to message my Page.

6

EXAMPLES OF SUCCESSFUL FACEBOOK ADS

The task of creating a successful Facebook ad may feel a little daunting if you haven't been trained in advertising. I know it was for me—I have an Engineering background, so I've had to overcome my nerdy roots and learn how to create ads that convert.

Your job as a new marketer is to watch Facebook ads in your feed and see what grabs your eye.

For the text in the ad, you can ask these questions:

- Is the text long or short?
- Are certain words jumping out, or are they using capitalization that catches your eye?
- Are they using emojis?
- What is the headline of the ad say?

Then for the images, watch what catches your eye the most:

- Are there people in the ad or is it a picture of something abstract?
- Do they have any text on the image?
- For video ads, what is grabbing your eye on the video?

Observe and watch what kind of engagement they have on the ad. Think of yourself as a detective getting new ideas for your own marketing. Remember that not every ad out there is successful, obviously - just because someone else is doing it doesn't mean it's working.

In the Taking Action section of this book, we are going to go step by step into the creation. But it's a good idea to get your images and text started before then so that you aren't creating that on the fly.

In the hour or less estimate, I mention spending **10 minutes on writing your ad.** You may want to write your ad in a Google Doc or Word Doc first so you don't lose your work and you can easily add variations to the text to test it. Write your Headline and the Text separately so that you can just copy and paste those into your ad when you are in the creation process.

ELEMENTS OF A SUCCESSFUL FACEBOOK AD

The biggest parts of a Facebook ad are the Image, the Headline, and the Text. There are other pieces to take into consideration (like the call to action button) but I find that these 3 parts are the most critical.

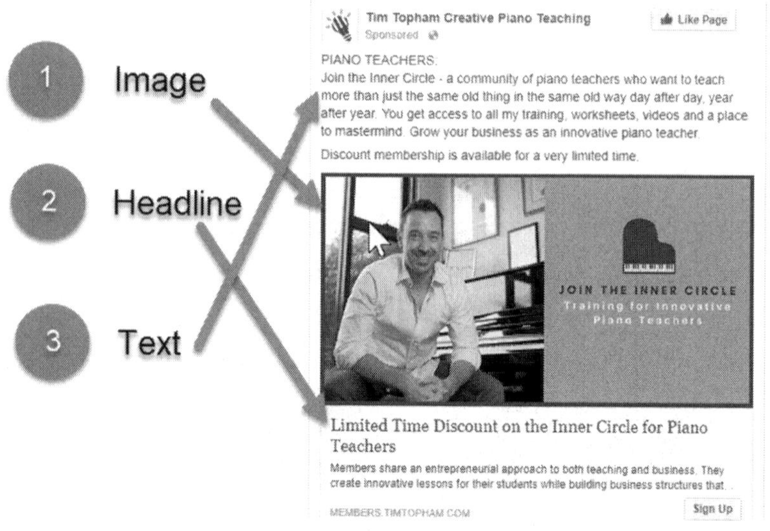

The Image is the most critical part because that is what is going to catch someone's eye first typically. Next is the Headline, which appears below the image and is the largest text. Then comes the text of the ad, which appears above the image. You could argue about which is more important, the text or the headline—they can both be powerful parts of your ad.

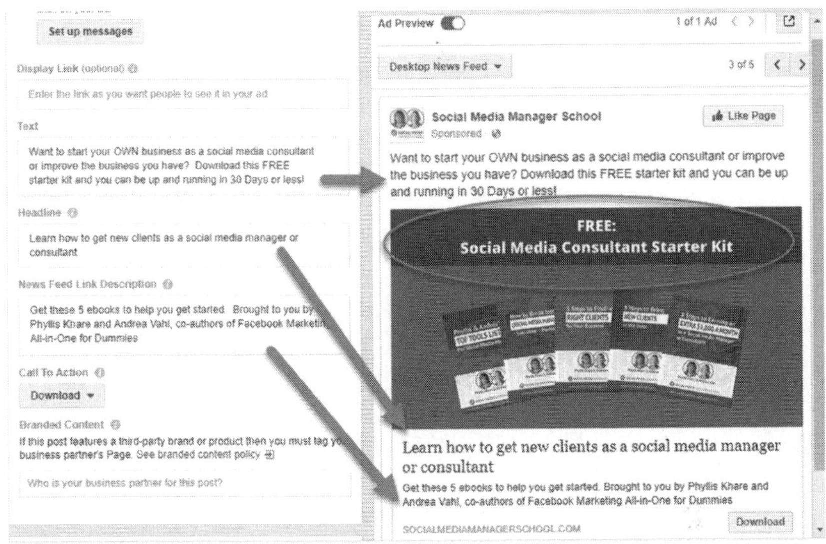

The News Feed Link Description isn't quite as important because it doesn't appear on mobile devices. But it can still be a good place to put some extra information.

Also, note that the image can be a good place to add some powerful text.

HOW TO WRITE A POWERFUL FACEBOOK AD

There is no one-size-fits-all approach to writing a powerful Facebook Ad. Sometimes shorter text can work, other times you may want to test longer text.

I like to approach writing ads with the traditional "Problem, Agitate, Solution" method. First, you present the problem that your potential customer is struggling with, then you agitate the issue, and finally present the solution. But there also can be nuances to this method in that you also want to establish a connection with them and showcase that you are an expert in the field. This all can be done in a short space or using longer copy.

Here is the formula:

1. Attention grabbing headline OR Thought-provoking question. For example: "Tired of figuring out dinner for your family?" or "MOMS: Stop the dinner planning now!"
2. Relate to them and tell them how you have been there
3. Introduce your qualifications or showcase why you are an expert
4. Tell them what you have that will solve this problem (bullet points, words that convert).
5. Paint the picture of the transformation your product will produce
6. Call to action to sign up

You can add these elements in different sections of the ad, they don't all have to be in the text section.

EXAMPLES OF FACEBOOK ADS IN DIFFERENT INDUSTRIES AND WHY THEY WORK

I am going to showcase a number of ads, but I'm also going to tell you that I'm not totally sure they all work. Some of these are examples from my clients, so I know they do work.

But others are ads that I've gathered that I "think" work because they have a lot of engagement and they are well structured. I don't know for sure that some of these are getting a good return for the advertiser. But my guess is that they are profitable because they continue to run the ads over time.

17HATS

17hats is a B2B software company that targets solopreneurs and consultants.

Why this ad works:

- They present and agitate the problem that consultants are dealing with when it comes to working with clients
- They show their expertise in the headline by mentioning Inc
- They offer a free trial to get people testing the software

1800FLOWERS

1800Flowers is a well-known company that delivers flowers and gifts.

Why this ad works:

- They have an eye-catching video
- They offer a big discount
- They paint the picture of the outcome people want—smile guarantee

BOULDER CAMERA

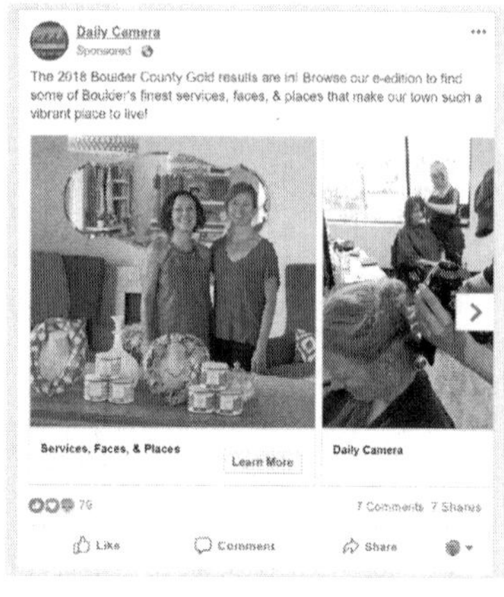

This is the local paper in Boulder that reviews businesses in their "Boulder County Gold" magazine.

Why this ad works:

- They have an eye-catching ad in Carousel format
- They offer a valuable resource to the local community
- They are featuring people in the images

CONSTANT CONTACT

Constant Contact is a B2B company that offers an email marketing system.

Why this ad works:

- They have person in the photo
- They offer a free trial with no credit card (which can be an objection people have to completing a free trial).

THRIVE CAUSEMETICS

Why this ad works:

- They have an eye-catching

video demonstrating the product
- They highlight the vegan and cruelty free feature
- The emphasize the benefit of a lash extension look with just the mascara

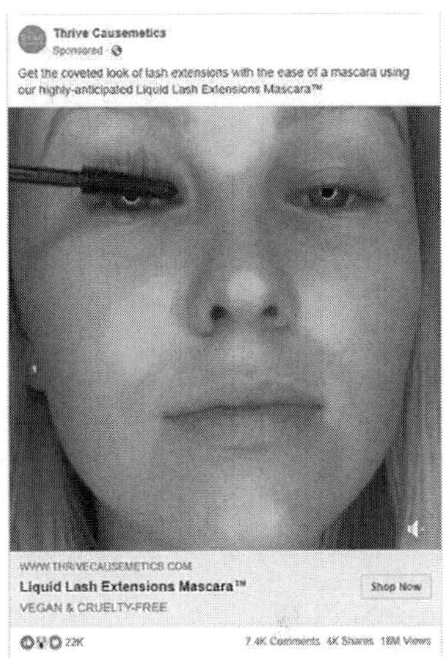

JADOT WINE

Louis Jadot is a French wine company looking to grow in the American market.

Why this ad works:

- They have an eye-catching image with a pop of color
- They offer a discount

SUE LARKEY

Sue Larkey is based in Australia and offers training for parents and teachers working with kids on the autism spectrum.

Why this ad works:

- She is using emojis to catch people's eye
- There is a free webinar that teaches valuable information to her market
- She is a big part of the brand and is featured in the image

VITAL ANIMALS

Vital Animal the Natural Path offers training on how to rear dogs naturally.

Why this ad works:

- The image of puppies catches people's eye (in fact, if you can get into a business that relates to puppies, I would highly recommend it—they get great click through rates, LOL)
- The ad agitates the pain of what can happen with immunizations
- The have a free offer for learning what to do about the problem

RESEARCHING FACEBOOK ADS

Finding successful Facebook ads is a challenge, because there isn't a "central" place to see other Facebook Ads. You can only see what is being targeted to your Facebook profile (which for me mostly seems to include wine and bra ads—my feed is a little frightening).

AdEspresso, a tool that helps you run Facebook Ad campaigns, has compiled a very interesting list of ads here: https://adespresso.com/ads-examples/.

Some of the things I look for on an ad to see how well it might be doing is the number of shares, likes and comments on the ad. These markers can be an indication of how long the ad has been running and how interesting it is to the people it's targeting.

You can now see the ads ANY Facebook Page is currently running by going to the Info and Ads section on their Facebook Page.

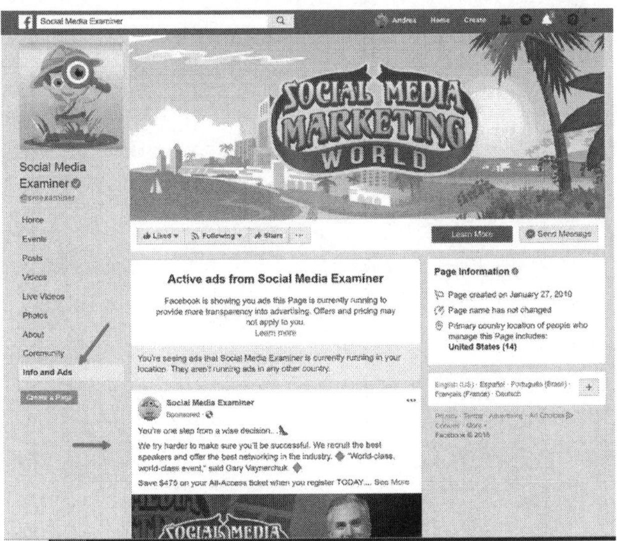

While this might feel invasive to marketers who are running ads, there are limitations that make this not as revealing as it appears.

What you can see:

- How many Facebook ads they are currently running
- What the ads look like
- Where they are running ads

What you can't see:

- The exact targeting of the ads (more on this in a bit)
- The budget of the ads
- How long they have been running
- The comments, reactions, and shares on the ads
- If the ads are successful

So there is a lot about the ad campaigns you can't know. But you can see if they are running a lot of the same images, then they are probably split testing their ads between many different targets.

The big takeaway from this chapter is to start watching other ads and get inspiration for your own campaigns. But don't just copy other marketers (because that's just rude). Do your own testing and experimenting.

7

INTRODUCTION TO THE FACEBOOK PIXEL

The mere mention of "Facebook Pixel" can strike fear into a non-techie marketer's heart. It sounds scary! Is it a thing? Do you have to order it from Facebook? Does installing it require a degree in computers?

I'm happy to report that it really isn't all that bad. There can be some hiccups or challenges depending on what type of website you have, but typically these challenges are easy to overcome.

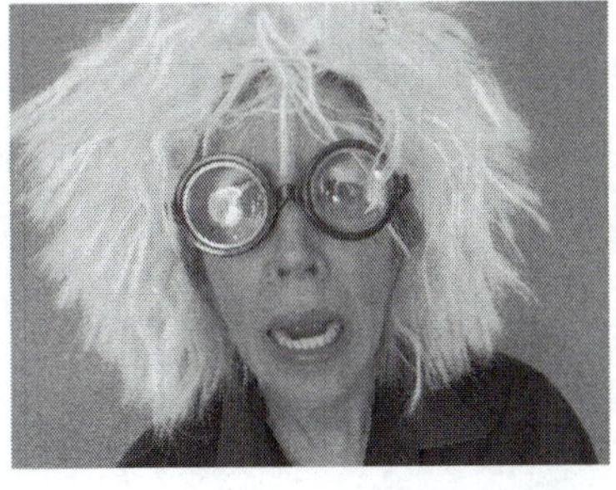

The Facebook pixel is TOTALLY optional. You can run Facebook ads just fine without the pixel. Don't let this stop you from getting started. BUT your ads and tracking will perform better with the Pixel installed on your website. So I do recommend spending a little bit of time if you can and getting the code on your website.

IMPORTANT CONCEPTS TO UNDERSTAND ABOUT THE PIXEL

First of all, what is a pixel? A pixel is just a bit of code (also known as a script) that you put on your website that sends messages back to Facebook for tracking purposes. You only have to install the base code one time before it starts working.

It's very similar to Google Analytics code, if you are familiar with that. The base Facebook Pixel code needs to be installed on your website just one time in the <head> </head> section of your website (there are a few methods of installing it that I will cover).

Each ad account only has one pixel code. You can install this pixel on multiple websites and then you can track those sites separately by using Custom Audiences. But you always use the same code that is associated with your ads account.

The audiences and tracking starts only after you install the code. So get the code installed as soon as possible if you want to target people who have visited your website.

The Facebook Pixel has two jobs:

- To track traffic on your site, which gives you the ability to "retarget" that traffic with an ad on Facebook
- To track conversions from an individual Facebook Ad and report those conversions in the Facebook Reports area

The first job of the pixel is easy to achieve. All you have to do is install the pixel to start tracking the traffic.

For the pixel to achieve the 2nd job, there is a little setup involved. You need to "tell" Facebook what a conversion looks like for you.

You can do this by installing an extra bit of code called a Standard Event in the location where the conversion happens OR you can create a Custom Conversion (more on this later in the advanced topics section).

A Custom Conversion is as simple as telling Facebook the address of the "Thank You Page" where the conversion happens. There is no extra code to install.

You have a MAXIMUM of 100 Custom Conversions that you can add to your account. You can delete them if you are not using them anymore but you cannot edit them.

You can place the Standard Event codes on unlimited number of web pages. So if you have lots of different conversions to track, you may want to focus on using the Standard Event codes (again, more on this later).

FIRST STEP: CREATE AND INSTALL THE FACEBOOK PIXEL

First, navigate to the Ads Manager at https://www.facebook.com/adsmanager/ or if your Ads Manager is inside the Business Manager the address is https://business.facebook.com/adsmanager/ and then follow these steps:

1. Click the 3 lines (a.k.a. the hamburger menu) in the upper left corner of your Facebook Ads Manager and select Pixels (you may have to select All Tools first on the left to expand the menu).

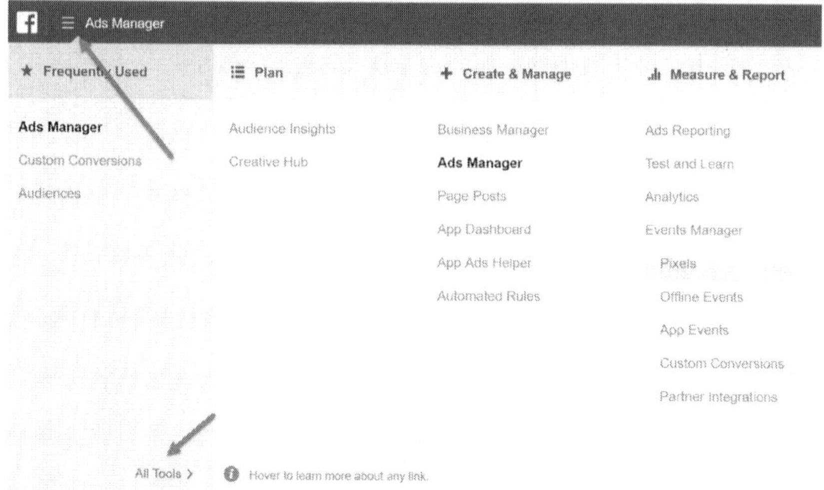

2. You should see that your Pixel is not created unless you have installed it before and you can select Get Started (this screen may look different for you, and the button may also say Create a Pixel). If you have already created the Pixel and it's tracking traffic, you'll see a graph on this screen.

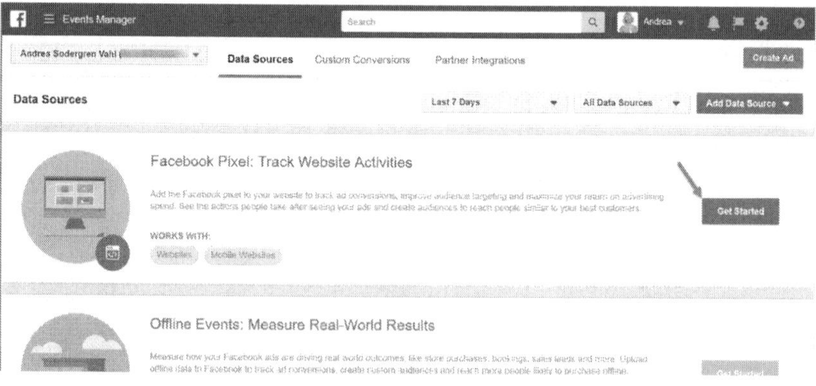

3. A popup box appears, and you can name the Pixel. The name doesn't matter that much other than during sharing and the name will not appear anywhere. Select Create.

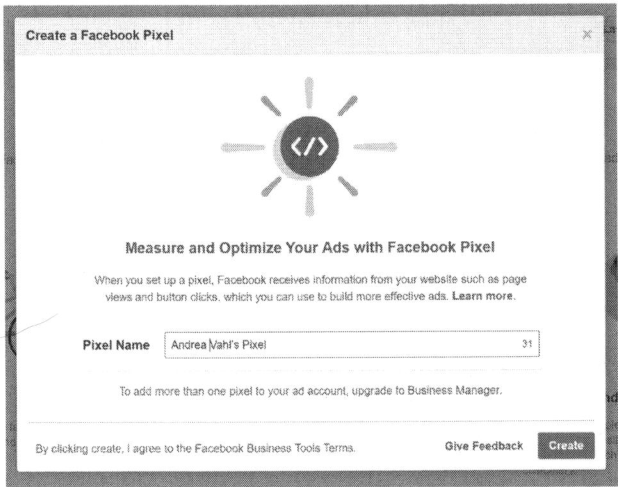

4. Another popup box appears and you can choose how you want to install your pixel. Integration or Google Tag Manager (there is also a plugin for WordPress), Manually Installing the Code Yourself, or Emailing the Instructions to a Developer (if you have someone who does your website maintenance). More information about Partner Integrations can be found here: https://www.facebook.com/events_manager/partner-integration. You can also find more information in your top menu under Partner Integrations just below the Pixel selection you chose earlier.

I can't go through all the options here, but one of the more common scenarios is downloading a WordPress plugin that you then upload to your Plugins area to install your Pixel. It's very easy. I will cover the manual method so you know what that looks like. And remember, you can put this Pixel code on other sites as well that have a spot for scripts (like Eventbrite, LeadPages, StealthSeminar, and more).

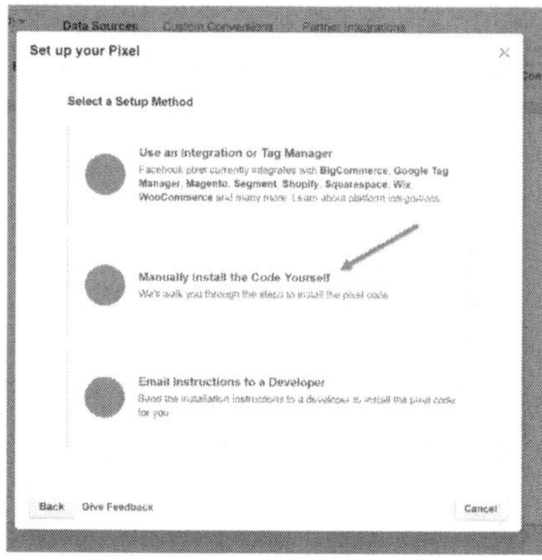

5. When you select Manually Install the Code Yourself, you see another popup box with code in the second section. Click on this code to copy it to your clipboard and select Continue. When you do that, you will also see another popup with some additional tracking code that you don't have to worry about just yet (that is the Standard Event tracking).

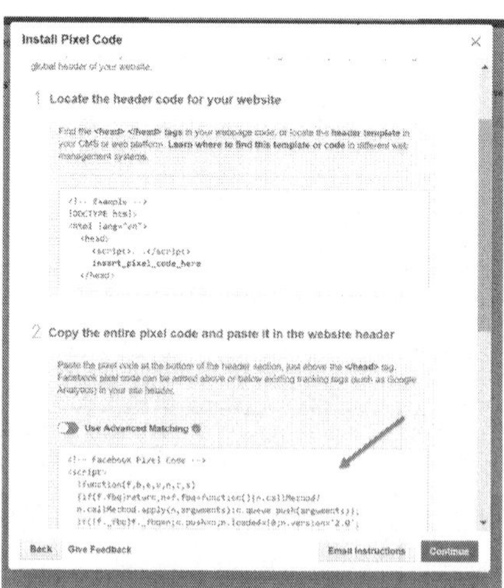

6. Go to your website and paste the code in between the

main <head> and </head> area. Some WordPress sites have themes that make this easier (a Header Script area) or you may have to go to the header.php file and edit that – typically under Appearance > Themes > Editor > Header.php. Get a webmaster to help you if you don't know where to find this.

7. You will know your code is working if you start to see some traffic recorded in the Pixel area. You may need to visit the site where the pixel was installed to "activate" the Pixel.

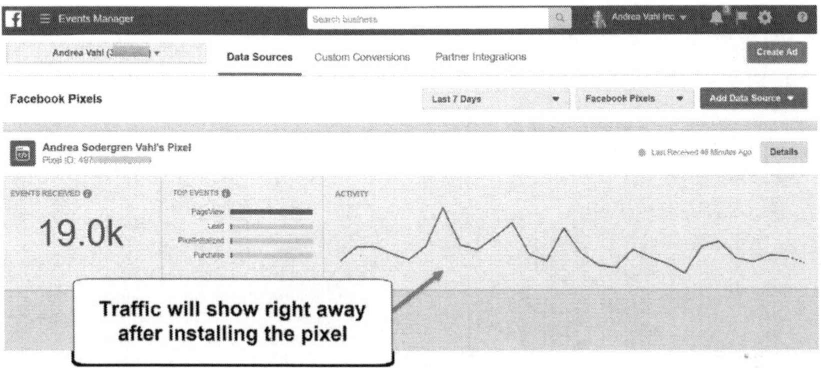

If you are not showing any traffic, use the Facebook Pixel Helper Chrome extension to help you troubleshoot the problem. You can install the Pixel Helper here:
https://chrome.google.com/webstore/detail/facebook-pixel-helper/fdgfkebogiimcoedlicjlajpkdmockpc?hl=en

I know that's a crazy-long website address, so just Google Facebook Pixel Helper Chrome and you will find the extension or do a search in your Extensions area on Chrome.

With the Facebook Pixel installed, you can also optimize your ads around Landing Page views rather than Link Clicks so that you know people are actually getting to your website rather than just clicking the link in the ad.

At this point, you are done with the Facebook Pixel installation. That's really all you need to do to start getting some of the benefits of extra tracking. See, that wasn't so bad was it?

But to go a little further and get a little more advanced, you would create a Conversion either with a Standard Event or a Custom Conversion. Then you would be able to optimize your ads around Conversions.

For now, we are going to keep things simple (hence the title of this book) and just create a Traffic ad in our Taking Action section. You will learn about Boosting a Post in the next chapter. The second step of using the Facebook Pixel (creating a Conversion) is covered in the Advanced section of the book. You'll also learn more about using the Pixel for Retargeting.

8

BOOSTING A POST - DO'S AND DON'TS

Are you using Boosted posts on Facebook? Wondering when you should boost a post and when you should create a Facebook ad using the Facebook Ads manager?

I used to not recommend boosting posts because of the way the post was optimized around getting engagement only. You couldn't reconnect with the people who have engaged with your post. But now with Facebook's "engagement retargeting" and the fact that you can optimize around driving traffic, the Boost post button is not a bad strategy.

In this chapter, you will learn some of the pros and cons for Boosting Facebook posts. You'll learn how to know you are boosting the RIGHT posts as well as when you should use the Facebook Ads manager to create your ad.

ADVANTAGES TO BOOSTING POSTS ON FACEBOOK

Let's face it, the #1 advantage is that it's EASY. In one click, and a couple of parameters you can push your message farther into the News Feed. Plus Facebook is constantly encouraging you to boost your posts. Maybe you've seen some of those messages - "Hey this post is doing better than 95% of your other posts, why don't you boost it? Do you want to boost it now? How about now?"

Boosting posts is essentially "Facebook lite" advertising and there are better options in the Ads Manager. But I still will boost my own posts and I do see sometimes that a boosted post out performs an ad created in Ads Manager. The key is to really compare the right metrics to know which type of ad is performing best.

To be effective in boosting your post, you must:

- Choose a post that has a benefit for you
- Wait at least a couple of hours to let that post get some organic reach and engagement
- Make sure that post is already doing well organically before deciding to boost it
- Optimize your Objective around your goal
- Add the proper targeting (I typically target my warm audience)
- Choose your budget and schedule
- Make sure you have the Facebook Pixel installed so you can capture traffic and track any conversions from your boosted posts (even though it's a boosted post you can still track a conversion to a sale or lead)

Finally you should always compare your stats and turn your boosted post off early if it isn't achieving your goals.

WHICH POSTS SHOULD BE BOOSTED ON FACEBOOK

Here's the tricky part, often people are not choosing the best posts to boost. If you choose a less engaging post to boost, you will get less reach and higher cost in advertising spend. As Larry Kim, founder of Mobile Monkey, says, "Only boost your unicorns, don't boost your donkeys." (See https://www.socialmediaexaminer.com/how-to-use-facebook-ads-to-boost-best-content/ for a recent interview)

Go into your Facebook Insights to see if your post is getting good engagement rate first. I typically only boost posts that have a 5% or higher engagement rate. But your engagement rate baseline may be different, so pay attention to your own stats to see what is "normal."

Engagement Rate is the percentage of people who interact with your post of those who have seen it. Basically, it's Interaction over Reach. Engagement rate "normalizes" the fact that each post gets different reach and allows you to really compare how a post is doing in comparison to other posts. You can make better decisions on how interesting a post is when you look at the Engagement Rate.

Here are the steps to see your Engagement Rate:

1. Go to your Facebook Page.
2. Click on Insights at the top of the Page.
3. Click on Posts on the left sidebar.

4. Click the down arrow on the right side under the graph and select Engagement Rate.

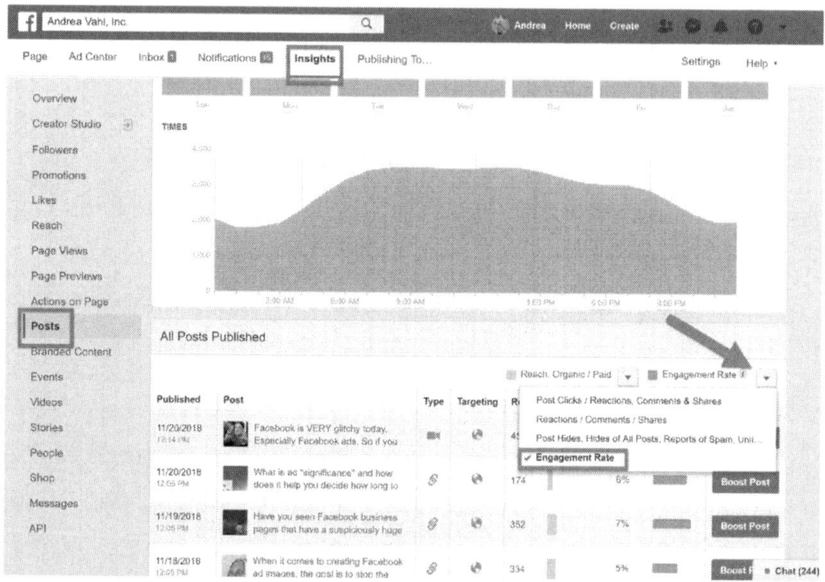

Typically, I only Boost posts that are doing well with 5% or more engagement but there are other reasons to Boost a post. For example, to get the word out about a promotion or blog post. But also consider the fact that you may want to create the ad from scratch rather than Boost the post so that you can optimize it in different ways.

LIMITATIONS TO BOOSTING POSTS

Boosting Posts is easy but not always ideal. And there are several limitations with boosting posts that make it a less desirable choice than creating an ad from scratch with the Ads Manager including:

- Currently you can't edit the photo that is pulled in when

you have a website link as the post - this feature changes on Facebook from time to time, so check your options

- You don't have quite as many targeting options as you do with the Ads Manager
- You can't optimize your ad to get more conversions if you have the Facebook Pixel installed
- You don't have as many placement options and budgeting choices

So while Boosting posts is easy and can be effective when done right, you should PRIMARILY be using the Facebook Ads Manager to run your ads on Facebook.

Facebook is recommending that only 10% of your budget be spent on Boosted Posts and 90% in the Ads Manager.

There may also be some indication that Facebook "watches" who uses the Ads Manager and uses more sophisticated ad strategies. Facebook hasn't completely confirmed how this may affect your ads but they are watching everything we do (creepy, right?).

Using the Facebook Ads Manager for 90% of your budget overall is pretty good rule of thumb. You may have larger promotional times where you spend a lot during a short period (I do have clients spending $5K a day on Facebook for 10 day stints). Then you would use Boosted posts in between promotions to keep your audience engaged.

Most of your overall budget should be used in optimizing your ads in your Ads Manager so that you are getting the right targeting and hitting your goals.

HOW TO BOOST A POST THE RIGHT WAY

When you Boost a post, you can set some general parameters with optimization, targeting and budget. Facebook sets some default parameters but you definitely want to adjust those.

Here are the steps to boosting your post:

1. Click the Boost Post button either directly from the post on your Page or in the Post Insights section. You will see a popup box and note that you can scroll to change the parameters on your Boosted Post.

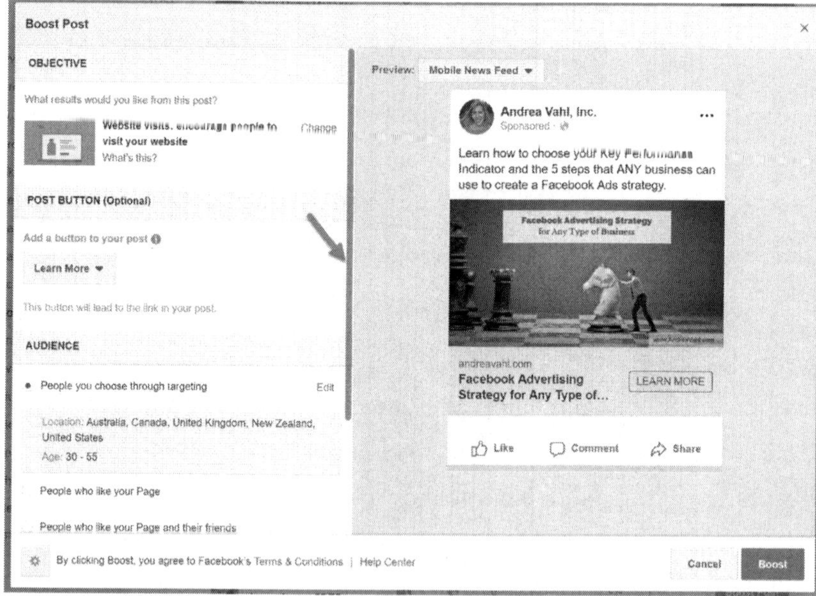

2. Select your Objective for your boosted post by clicking the Change link in the Objectives section (if you have a link in the post, you should select Website Visits).

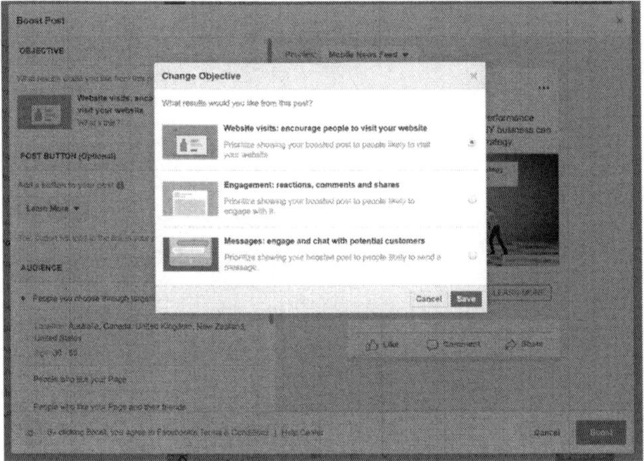

4. Adjust the Post Button by using the drop down menu if desired. Your choices are limited to Shop Now, Book Now, Learn More, Sign Up, Get Directions, Send Message or Send Whatsapp Message. These choices may change in the future.

5. Select your audience. This step is critical and often defaults to a very wide range or a selection you've used previously. If you have created Audiences in the Audiences section of the Facebook Ads Manager, those Audiences will be available here to select. That can be a great way to target your warm audience. Another good audience to select is the People who Like your Page, but that audience may be small. If you think the friends of your Fans would also be a good target audience, that selection could be good.

For example in this post, I have already created an Audience called "All Retargeting - emails video website engagement 25+ W US UK AUS CAN" so I can select that the boosted post target that audience. I could also see some of the other Audiences I've created or Create a New Audience.

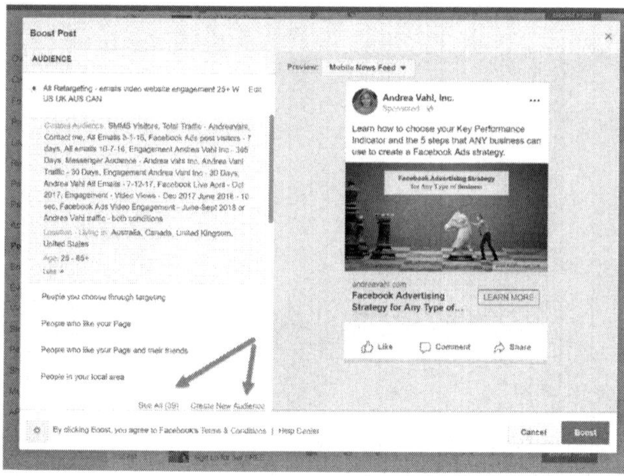

When I select Create New Audience, then I can target based on more general terms in the Detailed Targeting section.

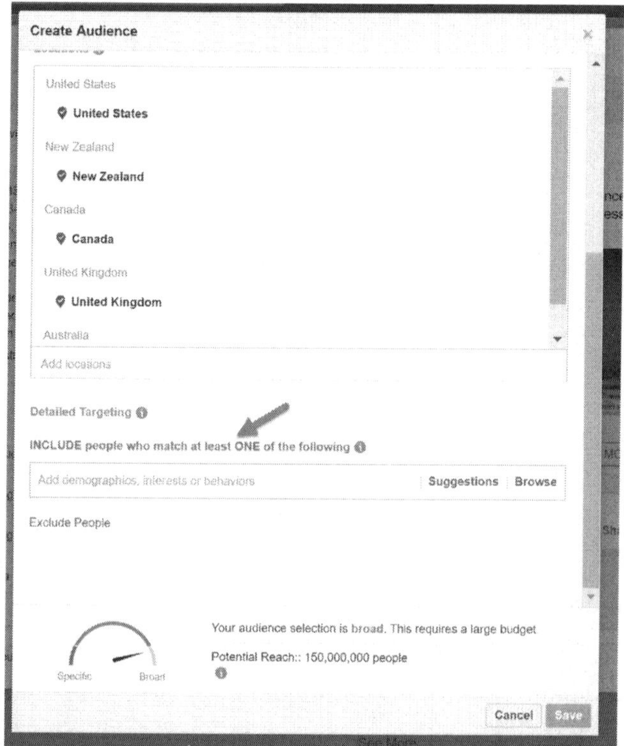

6. Choose the Budget and Duration. I typically choose $30 over 4-5 days but if you have a smaller audience you could just do $5 or $10. You will learn more about how to select budgets based on size later in this book.

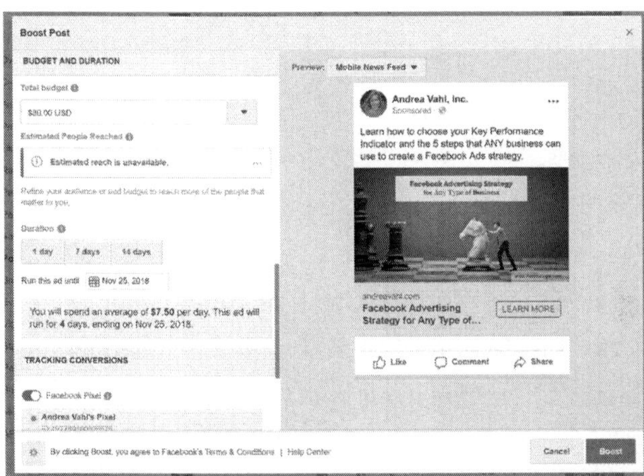

Also note that you can track conversions from a Boosted Post if you have the Facebook Pixel installed on your website. If you do have the Pixel installed on your website, make sure you have the "Tracking Conversions" set to on (green button is showing active).

7. Click the Boost button on the lower right corner of the popup—your ad will then go into a review process. Note that all the image requirements and terms and conditions still apply to any boosted post so your ad may get declined if it isn't complying with those guidelines.

Your Boosted Post will start running as soon as it goes through the review process. You will be able to see your results on the post itself but it's better to watch your results in the Facebook Ads Manager area because you get more information and details about the cost per click and other stats.

BOOSTED POSTS RESULTS IN FACEBOOK REPORTS

When your boosted post is running, you can see your results in 2 different places. One is by clicking on the View Results link or the button on the post itself. The View Results link or button may look different depending on if the ad is still running or if the promotion is complete.

When you click on View Results, you will see some of the stats that Facebook presents about what happened with the ad. Your results may look different depending on the Objective you selected as well as the configuration of your Facebook Pixel. You can see in this image that I was able to track Website Conversions because I had those Pixel events set up on my website.

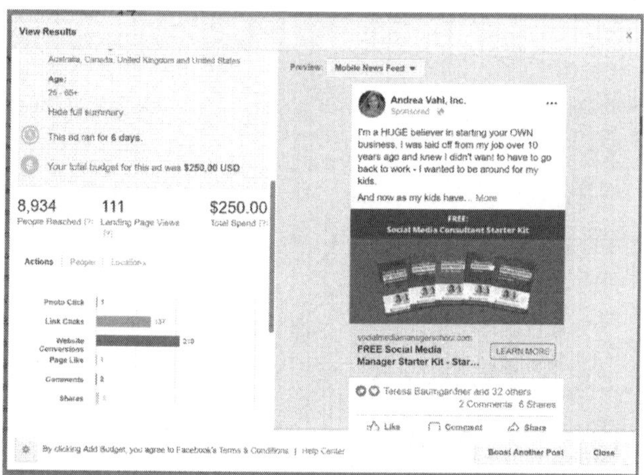

You also may notice that Facebook doesn't give you the cost per Landing Page View here so we would have to do that math in our head (yuck). That's why it's better to go into your Facebook Ads Manager and look at the reports.

When you go into the Ads Manager, you can see your named Ad campaigns or any Boosted Post there. The Boosted Posts are titled "Post:" and then the first part of the text you had in your Boosted Post.

Make sure you are customizing your Facebook Reports so that you see the right stats to compare your results (learn more about seeing up the Reports in the Taking Action section of this book). For example, I can see that the link click cost is $1.56 in the first ad which is a Boosted Post and in the second ad in this list the link click cost is $2.78. If I was trying to get the best link click cost, then I would be able to compare these ads equally with the report and know to shut down the ad that was more expensive.

I've been doing well with Boosted Posts as a traffic driver, and I can also get leads with those ads if people sign up for my newsletter if I have the call to action to do that in my blog post.

FACEBOOK BOOST POST STRATEGY SUMMARIZED

The Boost Post option is still a good type of ad to run overall, but you need to be smart about how you are using it. Here is my overall strategy that I use when I share a blog post on Facebook with the intention of using the Boost Post.

1. Write a blog post that I know will be helpful to my audience.
2. Create an image for my blog post that is eye catching and includes the title of the blog post in the image. Size the image properly for Facebook (for example 1200 x 628 or now a square image).
3. Make sure there is a call to action within the blog post to sign up for my email newsletter or get a free ebook so that people can get on my email list. I also have an exit popup on my website.
4. Post the link to my Facebook Page and wait a few hours for the post to gain some traction and get organic reach.
5. Make sure the post is doing well organically by checking the Engagement Rate in the Insights section.
6. Spend $30 boosting the post to Website visitors, Facebook Fans, and email subscribers ONLY in the locations of my most engaged audience. For me, this is US, UK, CAN, and AUS (it might be different for other people and you may not need to spend as much).
7. Make sure the Pixel tracking is on for the boosted post.
8. Uncheck the Instagram placement or Audience Networks placement (this can be checked by default and may be listed as "Automatic Placement").
9. Boost the post for 3-5 days, which would reach a significant portion of my warm audience for $30 (you may want to make this budget larger or smaller depending on the size of the audience you are targeting).
10. Watch the performance. If the ad isn't getting under $1.50/link click within $10 spend, then I shut the ad down early unless I really want exposure for that promotion.

For Boosted Posts, I'm getting better cost per website click because my warm audience is familiar with my content and wants to click over to read it. But for Conversion Ads, I typically get better conversion costs because the ad is optimized around trying to get a conversion.

BOOSTED POSTS DO'S SUMMARIZED

- Use Facebook Ads Manager for 90% of your ads budget and only boost to reconnect with your audience
- Optimize the look of the post before you decide to boost it by making sure the image and the text looks good
- Only boost posts that are already doing well in terms of engagement rate
- Wait at least a couple hours before boosting a post to let it get some organic reach and interaction
- Watch your stats in the reports area and turn off underperforming ads

BOOSTED POSTS DON'TS SUMMARIZED

- Don't boost your post on the Audience Network or Instagram. Always make sure you uncheck the Automatic placement for a boosted post. Automatic Placement can go to places like Instagram or the Audience Network and you typically won't get good results from other placements on a Boosted Post. Placing Instagram Ads is a great idea, just not with the boosted post option. I have found it doesn't drive traffic as well.

- Don't boost your post to an audience that won't respond well. Make sure you adjust your targeting and ideally boost your post to your warm audience.

Facebook Ads are extremely powerful, but the Boosted Post should not always be your first (or only) choice. Most of the time, you should probably be using a Traffic or Conversion ad with better targeting that you get through the Ads Manager.

9

CREATING YOUR FACEBOOK AD IMAGE

The image is the most important part of your Facebook Ad. Your image is going to be the biggest reason that people stop scrolling through their News Feed and click over to your website. You've seen people swiping through their News Feed quickly—and then all of a sudden stop and examine a post a little more. Maybe they click on it. Your goal is to Stop the Scroll.

Images with people usually do better than images with something more generic. If you are appealing to a certain type of customer, having an image that they will relate to – for example, when you are talking to carpenters and you've got a set of sweet looking hammers, they might stop and look at that.

It's a good idea to design your Facebook ad image before you start your ad, whether it's a boosted post or an ad you run through the Ads Manager. In this chapter, you will learn 4 tips to create eye-catching images that will improve your results.

In the hour or less estimate, I mention spending **10 minutes creating your image.** Your initial process may take a little more time as you get your system set up in Canva or the image tool you decide to use. Don't spend too long thinking about or researching stock images to use. Use a basic image and add some text to keep it simple.

TIP #1 – START WITH THE RIGHT SIZE

Different types of ads and objectives require different size images. Ahhh, Facebook. You LOVE to make things confusing, don't you?

Facebook also recently changed the sizing for the posts that have website links to allow square images rather than the "landscape" look they have used for a long time. But both sizes will work.

Image sizes are typically measured in pixels (no, it's not the Facebook Pixel we've been talking about previously). Pixel in this case is short for "picture element" and is used to standardize the measurements for computers and TVs. It's basically a dot on a computer screen.

Many programs for editing images give the size in pixels, which makes creating images easy. But if you have a picture that is a slightly wrong size, you will find that the image is cut off when you try to put it into an ad. You can crop and adjust the image in Facebook a little but you may not be able to get the image to appear the way you want.

The image size is typically given in terms of width then height. A common size that Facebook uses in their ads is 1200 x 628 pixels, which means 1200 pixels wide by 628 pixels high (although Facebook is now making a different size available in a 4:5 ratio—more on that in just a bit). If the image is square, then the commonly used pixel size is 1080 x 1080 pixels.

Sometimes the size is also given in a ratio that indicates each side of the image. A square image would be 1:1 meaning each side is the same size. Another ratio that Facebook often uses is 1:1.91 which means if the height of the image is 1000 pixels, then the width of the image would be 1910 pixels. But if you take the preferred pixel size of 1200 pixels and divide that by 628 you can see that you get the same 1:1.91 ratio.

Facebook also has a minimum size for ad images, typically 600 x 600 pixels. Images that are smaller will get a warning message that your image is too small to use in an ad.

Complicating the image equation are the new Instagram and Facebook Story placements that have vertical images and are sized at 1080 pixels wide and 1920 pixels tall.

Event ads and Like ads (under the Engagement objective) are sized slightly differently at 1200 x 444 pixels.

Is your head spinning yet? Let's make this a bit easier and condense this into a handy list of image sizes based on placement and/or image type:

- Images for the Facebook News Feed placement: 4:5 ratio (Facebook's new recommendation for images in the feed which would be 1080 x 1350 pixels) or 1:1 ratio which is 1080 x 1080 pixels.
- A long-standing ratio Facebook used to recommend was

1.91x1 ratio which was 1200 x 628 pixels (older dimension). Get more details here: https://www.facebook.com/business/help/103816146375741

- Instagram placement: 1080 x 1080 pixels
- Instagram Story or Facebook Story placement: 1080 x 1920 pixels
- Facebook Event or Facebook Like ad: 1200 x 444 pixels
- Carousel Ad: 1080 x 1080 pixels
- Slideshow video ad (uses up to 10 still images): 1080 x 1080 pixels or 1200 x 628 pixels (use same size for all images)
- Instant Experience also known as Canvas Ads: Variety of image sizes based on what elements you are adding into the ad. You can add Carousel ads at 1080 x 1080 as well as more vertical images of 1080 x 1920 pixels.
- 30MB maximum image size
- 600 pixel minimum width
- Best image formats .jpg and .png

Facebook will give you some guidelines in the image sizes when you create your ad.

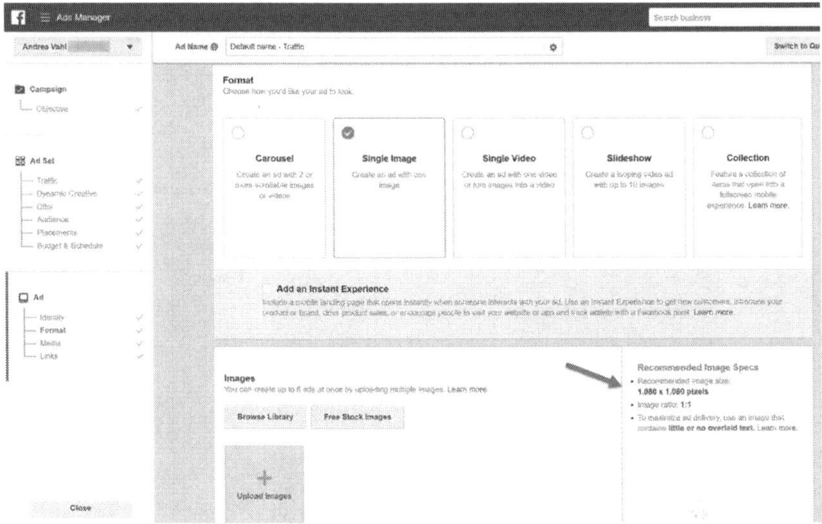

I use Canva (canva.com) to create the right sizes of images for Facebook Ads. Canva is a free online tool (that has some paid elements) and you can add text, frames and backgrounds to customize the image. Other good online image tools include PicMonkey, Adobe Spark (spark.adobe.com) and RelayThat.

One thing I like about Canva is the ability to keep multiple designs together. If you have a type of ad or image that does really well, you can duplicate it, adjust the text, or change that up a little bit, and then easily create a brand new variation of an image that you want to use again.

I use Canva to create my blog post images (that I will also use in boosted posts) as well as Facebook Ads. I typically start with either a stock image or one that I created, then add text to it. I try to keep the text large and readable for mobile ads while also keeping it to roughly 20% of the image.

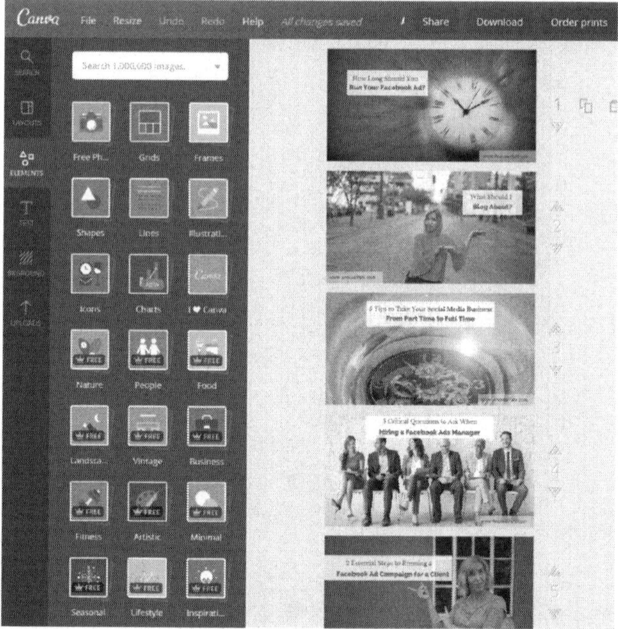

I use the Facebook ad dimensions for the featured image in my blog posts so that when I share it, it's already set up to look good on Facebook as well as go into an ad.

Canva has a way to select the Facebook Ad template when you create a design but it is set to 1200 x 628 pixels. So if you want one of the other dimensions, you can select Use Custom Dimensions and set the size you want to use.

TIP #2 – NOT TOO MUCH TEXT

One of the questions I get all the time is: Should we use text or no text in the images? I definitely find that having text in an image can help grab attention. But no text can sometimes make it look more like a regular post.

A while ago, Facebook had a strict 20% maximum text rule and your ad would not run if it had more than that. It officially "dropped" that limitation in 2016. But even though the rule is "officially" gone, Facebook will still stop ads that have too much text in them.

When you're uploading an image and you do have text on it, the high-text ads might even get a warning that your ad may not run and you should "Request a manual review." In general, I just place the ad as normal and then see how it goes. It is better to start with lower text images if you can.

You can use the Facebook Text Overlay tool to see what it says about the image before you place the ad. The text overlay tool is here: https://www.facebook.com/ads/tools/text_overlay. All you have to do is upload your image to have it checked by Facebook.

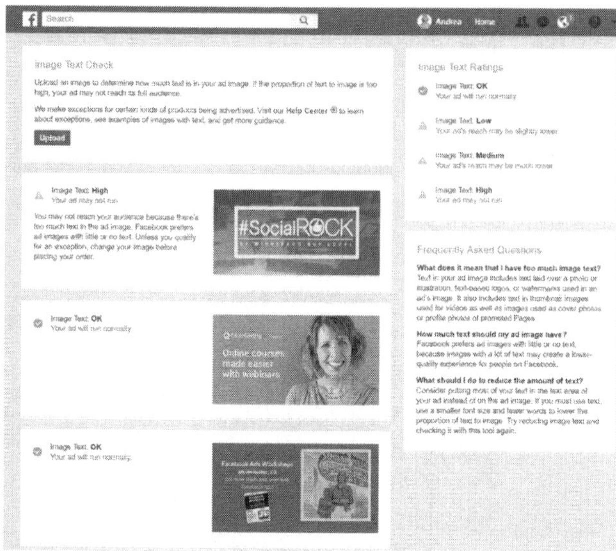

Text on book images or products or logos are not supposed to "count" in the text guidelines. But sometimes your ad will get disapproved anyway. If you are getting a warning and you've got images of books, go ahead and try to place that ad and you can appeal that decision if it doesn't get approved.

In 2016, I did an experiment to see if more text in ad images would change the results. Facebook threatens you with lower reach and higher cost to reach people, so that can be a concern. I uploaded several different types of ads with lots of text or little text, and I checked out the CPM (the cost per thousand impressions) and CPC on those ads.

I really found that my high-text ads did not do significantly better or worse. My medium-text ad gave me the best results in terms of cost per click and my high-text ad that gave me the best CPM, which is interesting since Facebook warns you otherwise. There are a lot of factors that go into ad performance and high text may not negatively affect your ad.

If you do have text, make sure the font is clear and the text is readable on desktop and mobile (if you are advertising on both).

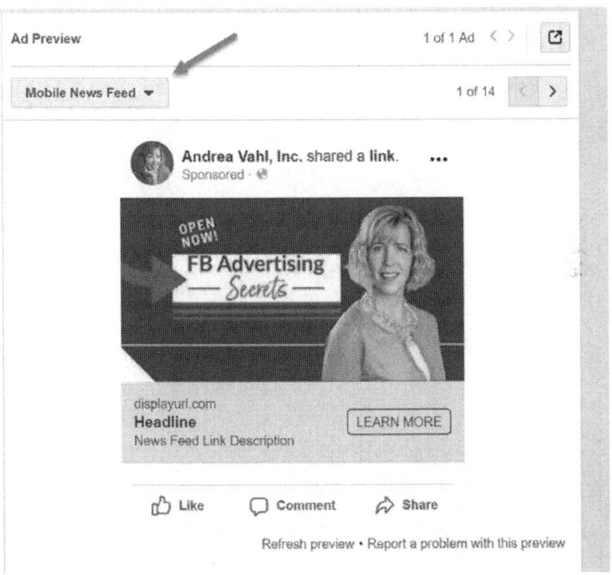

Or you can use images with no text and just an eye-catching image.

TIP #3 – USE AN IMAGE THAT CATCHES THE EYE

Whether you have some text in the ad, or no text, the base image you choose is critical. In general, images with people in them do better than objects, but that isn't always true. Remember that we are competing against posts from friends and family. We have to work hard to capture someone's attention.

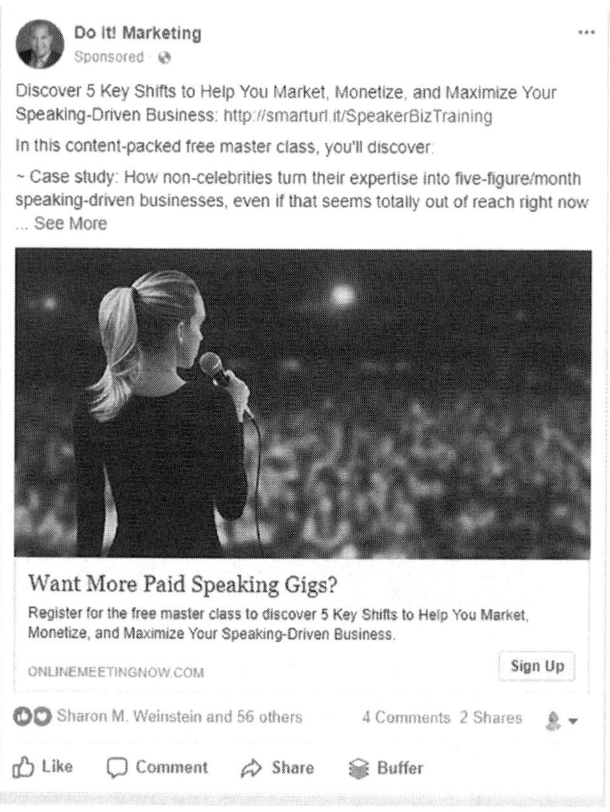

Also, I try to avoid overly cliché stock images. But at the same time, Facebook has some available free stock images that could work for you if you just want to get your ad started right away. These images are not able to be edited, but you can use them as an interesting image.

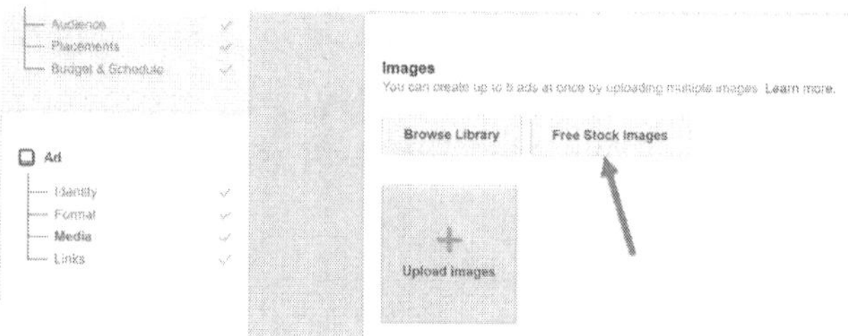

In the popup box that appears, add possible search terms in to find images that might be a fit for your ad. If these stock images are available, keep in mind that they may be used by other people (including your competitors) and they aren't unique to your brand.

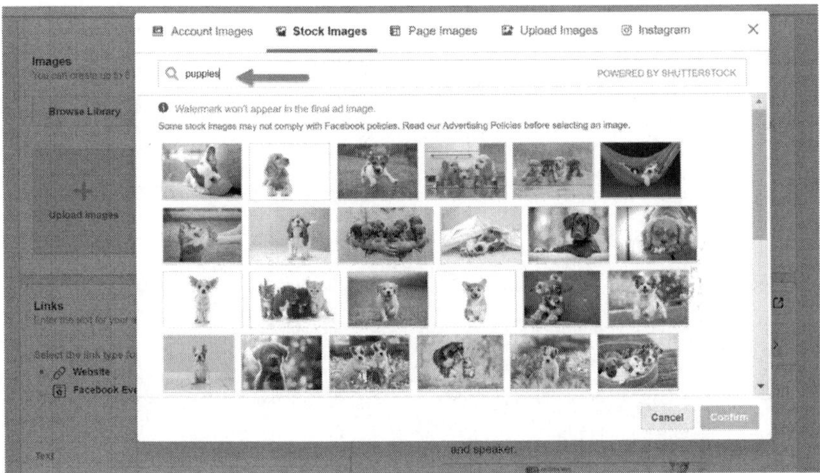

Some other good places to find images (both free and paid) are:

- Pixabay
- Pexels
- Depositphotos
- 123rf

My process for creating ads is to find a good image (or use a product image if you are advertising a product) then use Canva to add text that grabs attention and speaks to the audience. Once I've created the image in Canva, I download that image and then upload it into the Facebook ad.

TIP #4 – TEST DIFFERENT IMAGES

Split testing your Facebook ads is the key to really finding out which image works best. Your biggest difference in results is typically going to be from a different image or different demographics. When you test 2 different images, you will save money on one of the ads (occasionally they do perform the same, but more often you are saving money with one of the ads).

I often guess wrong on which image is going to do better. That's why you must test!

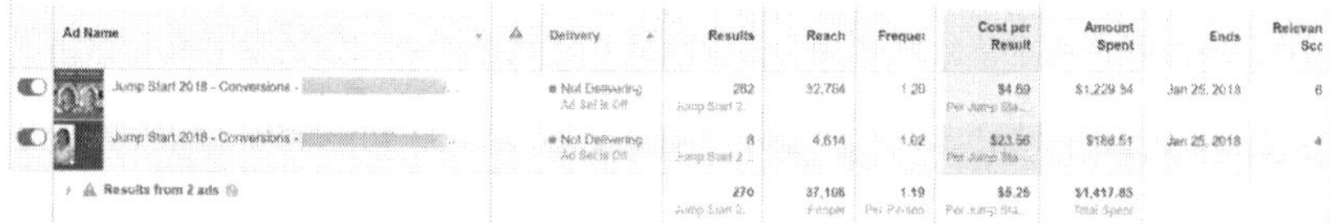

Ad Name	Delivery	Results	Reach	Frequen	Cost per Result	Amount Spent	Ends	Relevan Sco
Jump Start 2018 - Conversions -	Not Delivering Ad Set is Off	262 Jump Start 2...	32,764	1.20	$4.69 Per Jump Sta...	$1,229.34	Jan 25, 2018	6
Jump Start 2018 - Conversions -	Not Delivering Ad Set is Off	8 Jump Start 2...	4,614	1.02	$23.56 Per Jump Sta...	$188.51	Jan 25, 2018	4
Results from 2 ads		270 Jump Start 2...	37,108 People	1.19 Per Person	$5.25 Per Jump Sta...	$1,417.85 Total Spent		

In this example, the top image got 5x cheaper conversions than the bottom ad – all the targeting and the text were the same in each ad!

I didn't run the bottom ad as long, obviously. I didn't want to waste my money (and I probably should have stopped it earlier).

Good images are one of the biggest factors in the success of a Facebook ad and testing what works for you can put you on the path to better results! You will learn more about split testing in the Advanced Topics section, but keep this tactic in mind as you start creating images for your ads.

10

TARGETING YOUR AD: YOUR BIGGEST KEY TO SUCCESS

In the last chapter, you learned that the image in your Facebook ad is critical.

But the targeting that you choose will have the most impact on your ad's success. Because no image in the world is going to help if you aren't showing your ad to the right people. Sure, you may have some success. But that success may cost MUCH more than it needs to when you have the right targeting.

Before you go down the path of creating your ad, you should do a little research on what keywords are available and research your potential audience. Facebook is a little quirky because the keywords you can use are limited. You might know the perfect words to target, but those words aren't always available as choices.

In the hour or less estimate, I mention spending **15 minutes on research**. Your initial process may take a little more time as you learn about the tools available.

Don't spend too long overthinking your keywords! This can be a rabbit hole that can suck up too much of your time. List some of the good ones and pick which ones you will test first.

CUSTOMER AVATAR

You may already know your customer very well, but sometimes people say "Anyone is my customer." Um, no. Even if you are selling potato chips, you have a main target audience that buys your product.

When you target your ad to only your BEST possible audience, you will get better results. For example, in my Social Media Manager School course, men and women take the course. We have people in their 20s up to people in their 70s in there (love those people still learning!). But the majority of our members are 35-55 year old women, so that is who we target in our ads.

Your first step is to narrow your audience down to the best segment of your buyers. If you have a new product, then you may have to do a little guessing. You can also interview some of your first customers to find out more about them.

Think about your customer's demographics, their age, and where they live. Maybe they have a specific job title or an income level, or maybe they've attended a certain level of school. What kinds of interests do they have? What pages do they like? Where do they get their information from online? Write down their hobbies, clubs, food, books they read. What do they like to do? Not all of this might be relevant to your ad targeting, but the more you know, the better you will be at targeting your ad and crafting your message.

All of these characteristics come together as your customer "avatar." Here is a good list of characteristics to use in this exercise:

- Age range
- Gender
- Location
- Marital status
- Occupation/Job Title
- Level of Education
- Income Level
- Where do they get their information from? (websites they visit, books they read, podcasts they listen to)
- Goals (what they want)
- Challenges (what is stopping them)
- Objections (what reason might they give for not buying your product)
- What have they already done or tried to achieve their goal?

After you have a good picture of your current customers, you can research how to match that picture to the targeting that is available in Facebook Ads.

RESEARCHING YOUR AUDIENCE IN AUDIENCE INSIGHTS

The unfortunate message I have after you have created this wonderful picture of your audience is that not all of these keywords are available to use in Facebook ad targeting. Buzzkill.

And another big buzzkill is that Facebook has actually taken away some of the targeting that used to be available due to their privacy scandal in early 2018. But given those restrictions, you can still find some good keywords in the Audience Insights section of the Facebook Ads Manager.

Access the Audience Insights by going to your Facebook Ads Manager (click the down arrow in the upper right corner of Facebook and select Manage Ads) and then select Audience Insights from the menu in the upper left corner. Note that you may have to select All Tools in order to see the Audience Insights option.

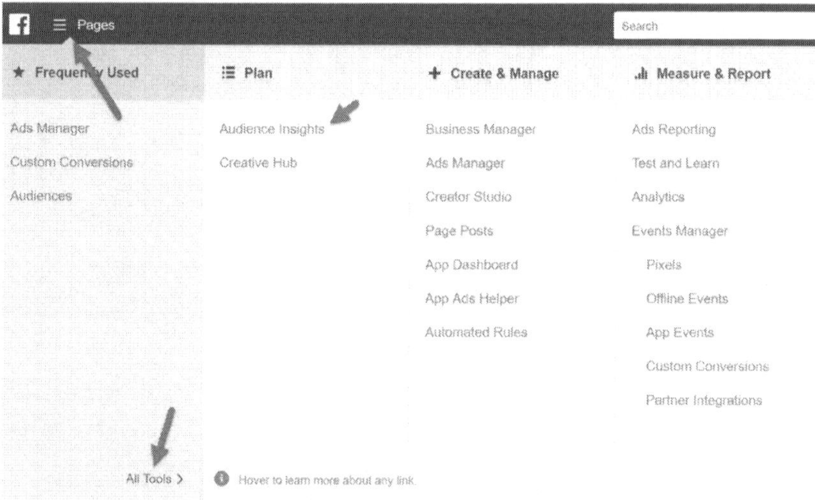

When you access Audience Insights, a popup appears and you choose if you want to analyze Everyone on Facebook or just People connected to your Page. If you have a larger Facebook Page (over roughly 2000 Likes), then you can analyze the people who Like your Page (recommended if you know that is a good core audience for you). Otherwise, you can choose Everyone on Facebook and we can add some additional keywords later.

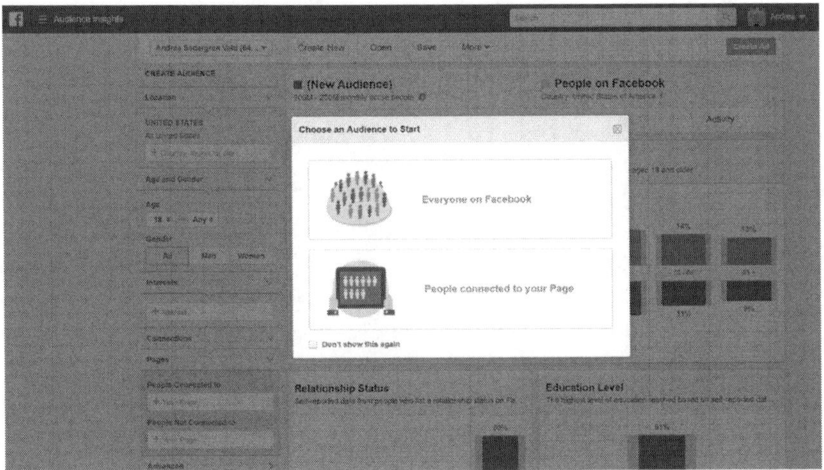

If you have a large enough Facebook Page, start your research there and select People connected to your Page. You will be prompted to put your Facebook Page in the Pages area on the left sidebar of the page.

When you select your Page, you can see some helpful things in the Demographics area including Age and Education Level. You can see that 81% of my Page Likes are from women in the 35-55 age range.

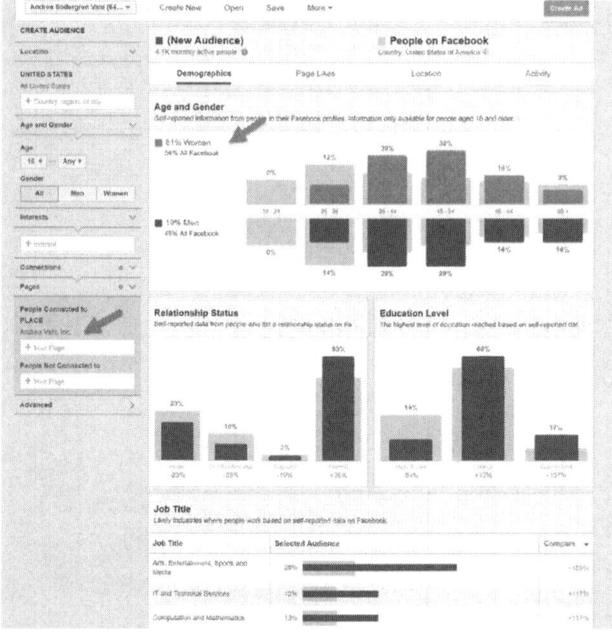

The most interesting section here is in the Page Likes section (one of the tabs at the top of the page), where you can see what other Pages the fans of my Page are interested in. Since you can target another Page's fans with Facebook ads, this is where you can get good keyword ideas.

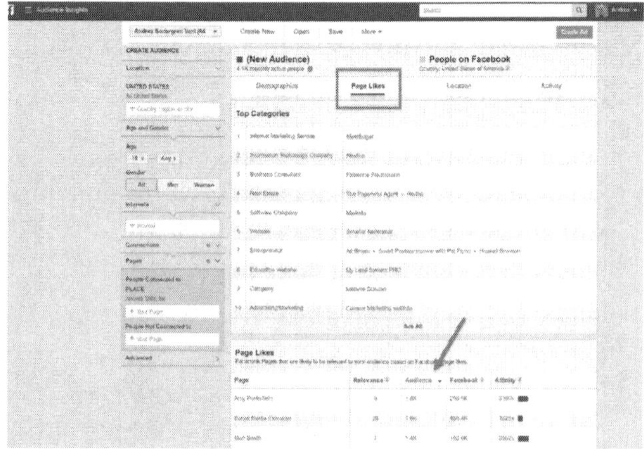

It has the Page Likes sorted by Top Categories, but at the bottom you can see the Pages sorted by Relevance. You can click on Audience to have the Pages sorted by the most number of people who also like that Page. My top keywords would be Amy Porterfield, Social Media Examiner, and Mari Smith (all keywords I successfully use).

The Audience Insights shows you a lot of potential Pages, but not all of them are going to be a good fit to target. For example, if you see a more general Page like Home Depot, your fans may like that Page but it wouldn't be a good potential target because it's too broad of an audience.

Also, **not all Facebook Pages are able to be targeted.** The reason some Pages can't be targeted is due to the size of the Page. But sometimes it's just hit and miss. Facebook doesn't let us know which Pages we can target and which we can't but I often see that a Page has to have around 50,000 Fans or more in order to come up as a possible keyword. Sometimes smaller Pages do come up, so it's worth testing.

MeetEdgar appears on my list of Pages in the Audience Insight section but it doesn't come up when I try to type that Page name into the Detailed Targeting section in the Facebook Ad area. But you can see that Social Media Examiner does come up as a keyword I can use. The only way to know for sure is to start typing the Page name in the Detailed Targeting area and see if it comes up as a word you can select.

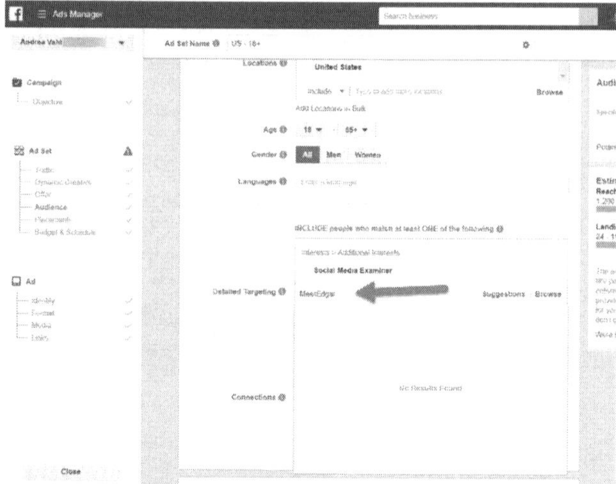

You can also do more research on keywords by analyzing Everyone on Facebook and then adding in keywords in the Interests section. For example, I could put another Facebook Page into the Interests section and analyze their audience (ooooh, powerful!) or I could put another more general keyword to see what types of Pages their audience is interested in.

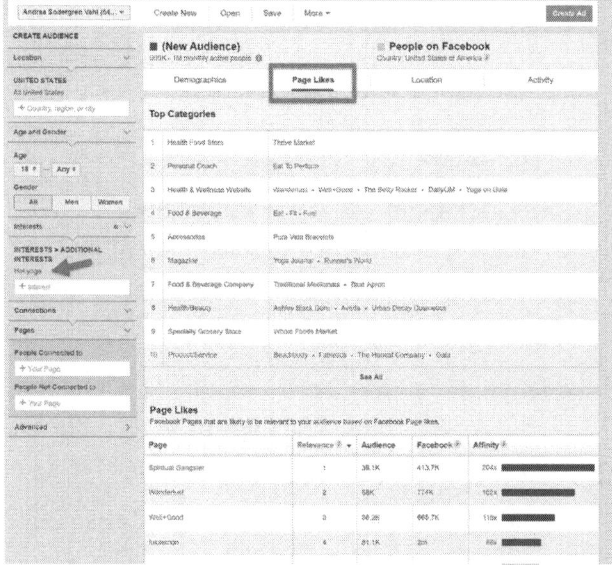

Be careful that you don't spend TOO much time on this activity. The important thing is to find a few good keywords to test and target. Next, we can use the Facebook Ads interface itself to do a little research into keywords.

DETAILED TARGETING SECTION IN FACEBOOK ADS

Once you have some ideas of keywords, you need to do a little research in the Detailed Targeting section of the Facebook Ads Manager. The Detailed Targeting section allows you to choose keywords. But the interesting thing is that Facebook doesn't tell you EXACTLY how they get to these keywords.

These detailed targeting options may be based on (according to Facebook):

- Ads they click

- Pages they engage with
- Activities people engage in on and off Facebook. This is related to things like their device usage, purchase behaviors or intents and travel preferences
- Demographics like age, gender and location
- The mobile device they use and the speed of their network connection

To access the Detailed Targeting section to do some initial research, you need to begin the ad creation process by going to the Ads Manager (if you are in the Audience Insights you can click the 3 lines in the upper left corner and select Ads Manager from the menu). Select the green Create button to start creating an ad. You can also go directly into the Facebook Ads Creation process by going to https://www.facebook.com/adsmanager/creation.

From here, just choose any objective like Traffic to get the ad started so you can get to the Audience section. Then just scroll down to the Audience section (in the Ad Set level).

The most interesting part of the Audience section is the Detailed Targeting. That is where you can target the Fans of other Pages, job titles, and interests. You can type in a keyword or Page name to see what types of matches come up.

In this example, Human Resources shows up as an Interest. This means that someone may have liked a Page that is related to Human Resources. If you are trying to target people who actually DO human resources as a job, you should focus on the Job Title targeting.

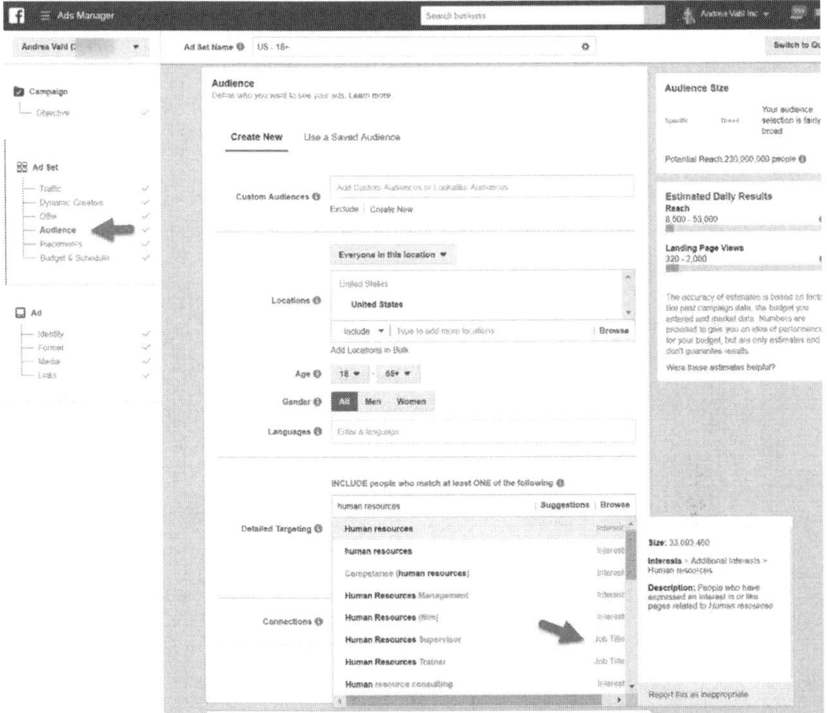

You can also see how many people are "in" that keyword category. So the top selection of "Human Resources" has over 33 million people in it, which is extremely broad. And you'll notice there is a slightly different variation just below it called "human resources." Unfortunately, we don't know exactly how Facebook assembles these categories. Jerks.

What we have to do is test the keywords to know how well they might work for us.

The other thing you can do is select multiple keywords in one target audience. BUT be careful with this practice. **One of the big mistakes I see people making is choosing lots and lots of keywords until their audience is too big!**

Facebook will not tell you which keywords are converting the best for you. So you may be wasting your money on bad keywords that don't give you results.

The only way to test keywords completely is to test them individually. Which is a lot of work, granted! I have some best practices listed later. But let me also tell you some of the cool things that are available in the targeting area.

- Target your ads to the fans of another Facebook Page (only available for larger Pages but sometimes available for smaller Pages - just start typing the Page name to see if it matches)
- Target your Ads to multiple interests - add keywords in the Detailed Targeting section
- Do complex matching to target your ads to people who have a certain interest AND another interest. For example, if they like Yoga AND Jogging (crazy people)

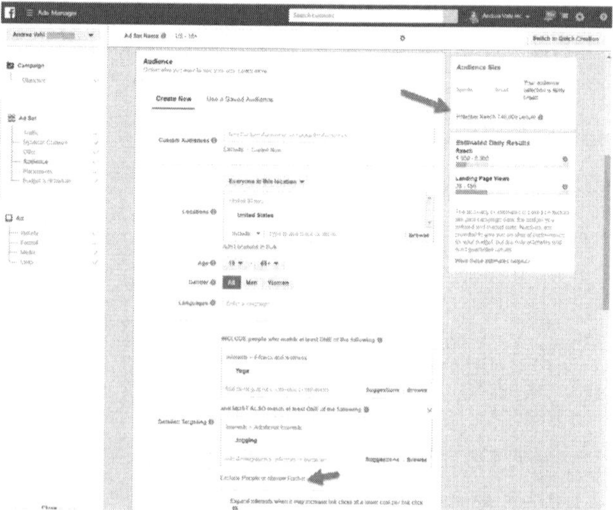

- Exclude certain interests to eliminate people. For example, you can target people who like Zillow except for people with the job title of Realtor (that allows you to advertise to potential people who are interested in moving without sending your ads to Realtors).

To do some of the complex targeting, you do need to understand how the Detailed Targeting section works.

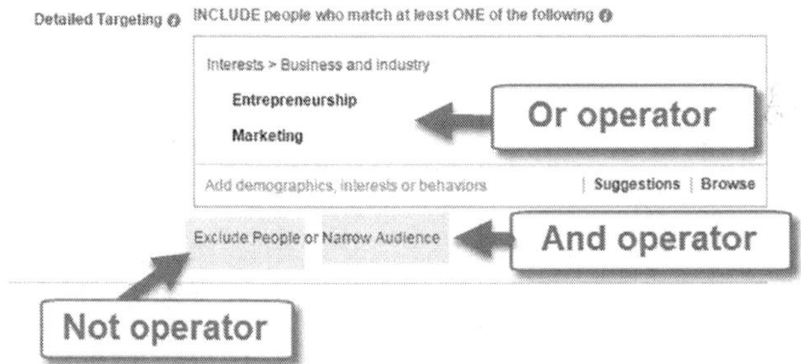

Once you put a keyword in, you can add additional keywords and that means the audience EXPANDS. So it's Entrepreneurship OR Marketing. If you Narrow your Audience that would mean any keyword you add there would be "Entrepreneurship or Marketing "AND whatever keyword you added so they would have to like both. If you clicked Exclude People, then you would say they couldn't be interested in whatever keyword you added there.

The Detailed Targeting section is EXTREMELY powerful. But don't narrow your audience too far or your ad won't get enough traction. It's better to keep your targeting a little more open and let the ad text and image appeal to your audience.

The other thing you can do to research possible keywords is to use Facebook's Suggestions tool. First, add a keyword and click

Suggestions to see what other keywords Facebook thinks might be similar. An example using the Zillow keyword, when you click Suggestions you can see lots of other potential keywords that might be a good fit. Again, beware of going too broad.

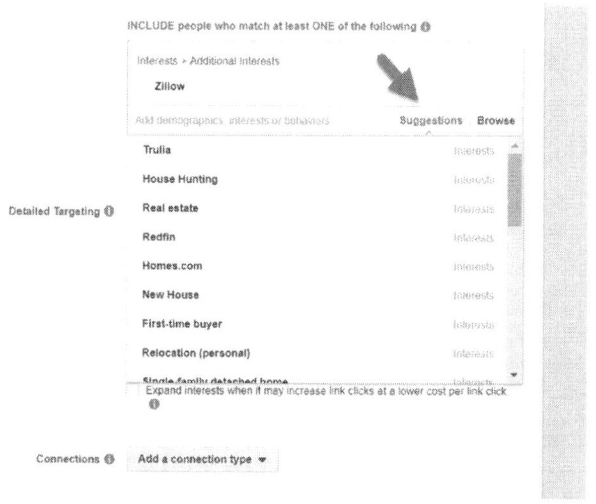

You can also look at the Browse feature to see specific ways you can target different Behaviors Facebook tracks. For example, you can target people who are Facebook Page admins of particular industries for a B2B application.

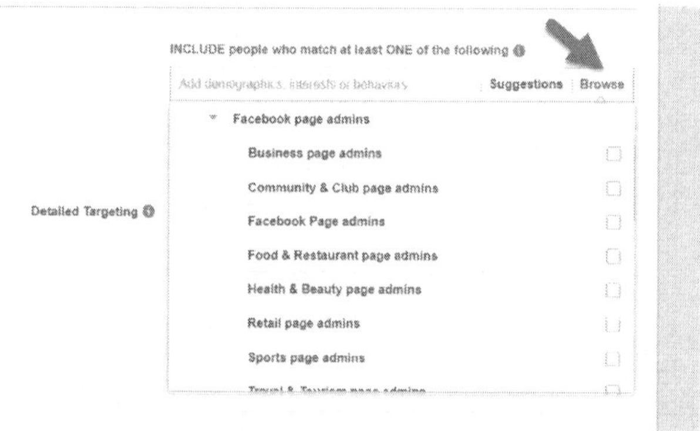

There are other possible behaviors in this section, as well such as Engaged Shoppers, Mobile Device Users, Frequent Travelers and more. The key is to test a variety of targeting options to see what works for you.

One of the other options in the Targeting section is the Expand Interests checkbox. You can select to Expand your targeting audience so that Facebook can adjust your interest-based targeting to reach more people who may get you cheaper clicks or conversions.

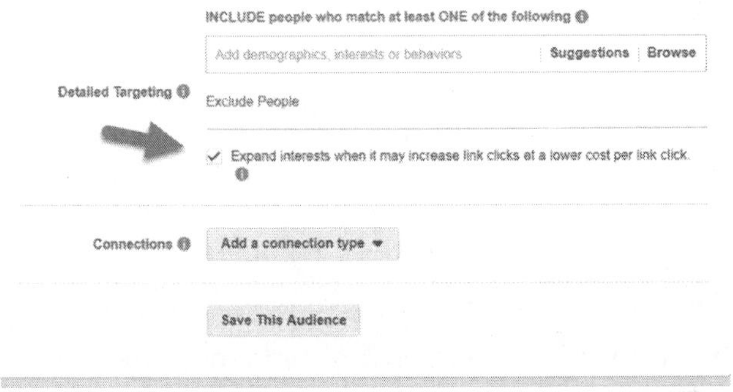

I've had this option work well in some cases and not as well in others, which makes this feature a challenge to recommend. I would consider testing both options. But in general, I think it can be good to **keep the Expand interests box OFF**. I've seen others who have also had worse results with the expansion box checked compared to when they have left the box unchecked and just used the targeting they had selected.

TARGETING BEST PRACTICES

You may be wondering just HOW you are going to choose from all these amazing keywords! How many do you choose and how do you know what's working? Facebook ads are 1 part science and 1 part art. And that is where testing comes in. You'll learn all about split testing in the Advanced Topics section. But for now, I have some best practices for you.

#1 KEEP THE AUDIENCE SIZE LARGE (BETWEEN 500K AND 2 MILLION) IN YOUR INITIAL TEST IF POSSIBLE

If you don't have the perfect keywords, then it's a good idea to not go too narrow or too wide from the start. You don't want to target 34 million people, but you also don't want to target 10,000 because your ad may not perform that well. Try to have a large enough audience so that Facebook can deliver your ad out to a wide group but still be optimized to reach people who are most interested.

You can see exactly how many people your keywords are going to reach in the Potential Reach area to the right of the targeting section. If you are a local business or if you already know your perfect keywords, then you don't have to artificially inflate the Potential Reach. This range is my suggestion based on years of testing.

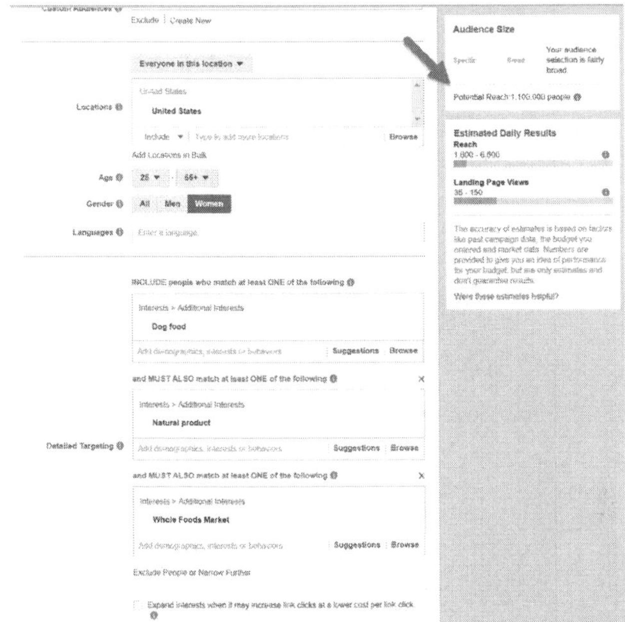

#2 USE SIMILAR GROUPS OF KEYWORDS IN ONE AD

If you are going to do additional testing (and I suggest that you do), keep similar types of keywords in one ad. For example, test all the job titles in one ad and similar Facebook Pages in another ad and maybe more general keywords in a different ad.

#3 IF YOU DO HAVE A SMALL AUDIENCE, DON'T OVERSPEND

This is more of a budgeting tip. But if you are targeting a small audience, you don't have to spend as much money to reach them. You typically can't target smaller than 1000 people. Sometimes Facebook lets it through, but often they won't allow you to even place the ad. You will learn more on this in the next chapter on budgeting.

Ultimately, good targeting comes down to testing. Don't get discouraged if you don't see the results you want with the first ad you run! Just test again with some different keywords or different ads. I know this might feel like a lot of work initially, but the more intentional you can be about your ad the better your results will be from the start. Once you've done this research once, your ad process will go smoother for the next ads you place.

In Chapter 17 in the Advanced Topics section, you will learn about Custom Audiences and Retargeting which is also extremely powerful!

Don't forget to grab your FREE live demo video and other resources that will help with this book at www.andreavahl.com/book-resources.

11

DECIDING ON YOUR FACEBOOK ADS BUDGET

Are you excited to start your ad yet? I know this has been a lot of background information, but some of these decisions are best made ahead of time. Don't worry, we are going to get your ad kicked off in the very next chapter, woohoo!

How much you should spend on your Facebook ad is one of the questions I'm asked most often. There is a lot to unpack here.

Different aspects of setting your Facebook Ads budget:

- Allocating how much you should spend on Facebook Ads vs. other parts of your marketing
- Determining how much to spend on your ads to be effective. Is there a minimum before you see a return on your investment?
- How to actually choose your Budget and Scheduling settings in the Facebook Ads manager

In this chapter, I'll touch on aspects of the first two points and then dive into choosing your budget settings.

YOUR OVERALL MARKETING BUDGET

The first thing you need to think about is the percentage of your budget you are spending on marketing and advertising overall. The Small Business Administration suggests that small businesses (under $5 Million in revenue) allocate 7-8 % of revenues to marketing. You may want to adjust this figure depending on if you are launching a product or just starting your business.

Once you have the overall marketing budget, determine how much of that marketing budget will go to Facebook ads. Obviously this might change depending on how effective the Facebook ads are for your business.

So let's look at the example of a small business making $100,000 in revenue. I work with a lot of solopreneurs and small businesses, and the budget question is often a big issue.

MARKETING BUDGET EXAMPLE

- Revenue: $100,000
- Total Marketing Budget: 8% = $8000
- Advertising Budget: 50% of total Marketing = $4000
- Facebook Advertising: 25% of total Advertising = $1000

This is just one example, and your business may be totally different as far as where you need to spend your money. But it's a place to start. Personally, my business focus is more online (and of course more on Facebook) so I typically allocate 75% or more of my advertising budget to Facebook ads.

So in this example, you have $83/month to spend on Facebook ads, which isn't a lot of money. But again, it's a place to start.

HOW MUCH YOU NEED TO SPEND ON FACEBOOK ADS

Many people ask if there is a "minimum" you need to spend on Facebook ads in order to see a return. The answer is no, but it depends on your niche and your goals. I've seen some people get lead conversions and sales right away. Other businesses take some time to test.

Also, think about how much a lead or traffic to your website is worth to you. A lead for a realtor selling a new home may cost a lot more than a lead for an online course that costs $500. But of course, the payoff for the Realtor is much higher if they convert that lead into a home buyer.

In the testing phase, you need to think about the significance of your results. It's hard to tell if an ad is successful if it's only had a few clicks on it. When you are choosing a budget, I usually suggest spending at least $25 to $50 per ad during the testing phase so you get some significant results. I also suggest spreading out the budget during the testing phase over 4-5 days so that the ad can optimize.

Once you have tested your first ads, you can decide if you are getting the results you want and then ramp up the spending from there. You can also visit the chapter on Typical Results to see how your ad is comparing to other industry numbers.

Another consideration when looking at spending and daily budget is the size of the audience you have chosen and your Estimated Daily Results. If you have a more defined audience, you don't want to spend more than you need. Remember that not everyone logs on every day (gasp —how could they take a day off?).

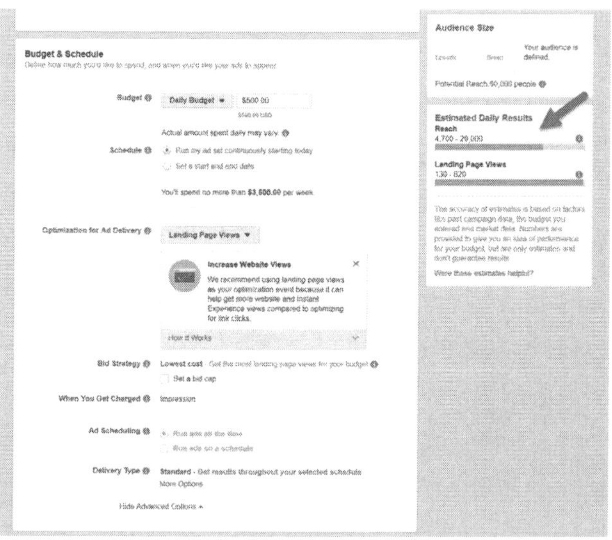

If your Estimated Daily Results are 50% of the audience you've selected, then you will probably be showing your ad to the same people over and over. Having people see your ad a couple times isn't a bad thing but you don't want people to burn out quickly from repeated views of your ad.

Once you have your targeting defined, take into account the Estimated Daily Results when you set your budget. I like to keep this figure at 25-30% or less of the full target number. You can also watch the Frequency in your Facebook Ad reports to make sure the number of times people are seeing the ad isn't too high.

OVERALL FACEBOOK ADS BUDGET RECOMMENDATIONS

The Facebook Ads budget and schedule section is at the Ad Set level in the Facebook Ads Manager.

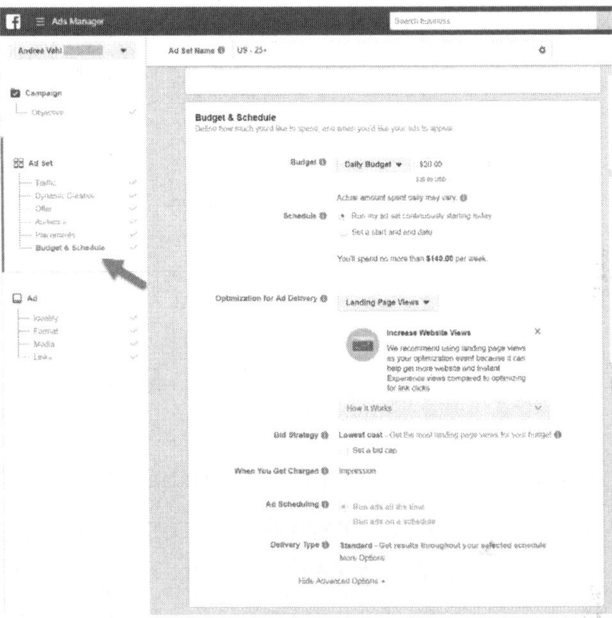

Your first setting option in the drop down menu at the top is Daily Budget or Lifetime Budget. The default is Daily Budget, and the ad spend is focused on hitting those set numbers each day where a Lifetime Budget allows for a little more uneven spending over your schedule you set.

Either one is fine but you will not be able to change your choice after the campaign is running. Here are some of the differences between the Daily budget and Lifetime budget:

Daily Budget:

- Set the amount spent every day, and Facebook tries to go through your budget each day
- Open ended schedule - you can set a begin and and end date to the campaign, but you don't have to set the end date if you want the ad to keep running until you manually shut it off

---

Lifetime Budget:

- Uses the total ad amount you set and may increase or decrease the average daily spend depending on the results but you will never spend more than the full set budget
- You must set a begin and end date to the campaign. If you want to keep the campaign going, you have to extend the end date and add more to the budget
- With a Lifetime budget you can choose to deliver your ad only during set hours of the day - for example, you could only show your ad during your office hours of 8am - 5pm

---

In general, I typically choose Daily Budget because it is easier to extend the ad campaign.

The next setting is the Schedule for the ad and you can set your start and end day. Setting the end day ensures that you don't accidentally leave your ad running - I've heard some horror stories about giant ad bills, and Facebook isn't very sympathetic!

The Optimization for Ad Delivery section is based on your campaign goal at the default setting, but you can change the optimization from the drop down menu.

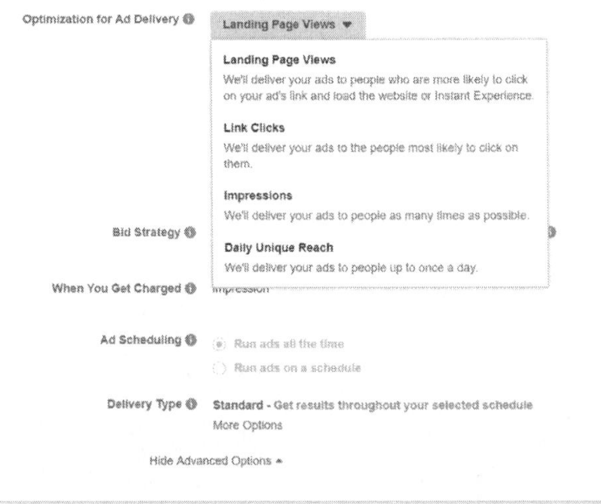

In this example, I have chosen Traffic as the Campaign objective. Landing Page Views is an optimization that you can only choose if you have the Facebook Pixel installed. Landing Page Views means that people actually wait for the website to load rather than click the link and maybe hit the back button before they see your website. Facebook tracks everything we do and knows the type of people who are more likely to actually wait for the Landing Page vs. people who might just click on the link (creepy, right?)

Facebook will try to show your ad more prominently to the type of people who you choose to optimize towards within the targeting you have already selected. So for example, if you have chosen to show your ad to people who like Yoga but you are optimizing around Conversions, then Facebook will find the people in that target keyword (Yoga) who also are more likely to convert.

For beginners, keep this optimization at the default setting. I typically don't change it at all but there are reasons you might want to show your ad to people just once per day (Daily Unique Reach) or optimize the ad in a different way.

The next section is the Bid Strategy, which defaults to Lowest cost. Facebook will work to get you the lowest cost for your objective. You can choose a Bid Cap, but if you choose too low then your ad will not show at all because other people are "bidding" higher to show their ads. Setting a bid cap is better for more advanced users who might be working with high volume ads.

The Ad Scheduling section is available if you have chosen a Lifetime Budget. This is where you can choose to show your ad at certain times of the day.

Delivery Type is also for more advanced users, or for people who need an accelerated delivery of their ads rather than a schedule.

BUDGET AND SCHEDULE BEST PRACTICES RECAP

For a recap, here are my best practices for budgeting and scheduling:

- During the testing phase, spend at least $25-50 per ad
- Run the ad at least 3-4 days to give it time to optimize
- Keep the optimization for ad delivery in the Default settings unless you have a specific reason to change it
- Don't overspend for the amount of Reach you have

Setting your Facebook Ads Budget during the testing phase isn't too complicated. You'll find which ads perform the best and you can scale those ads up and continue to run them.

Woohoo! Next up is our full walk through of setting up an ad from start to finish. I promise it will be MUCH easier and quicker now that you have some background on what everything means!

12

CREATING A HIGH-CONVERTING AD

Yes, you made it! In this chapter we are actually going to walk through step-by-step and create a Facebook ad from scratch! All the background work you've done will help you get this done in 30 minutes or less. And if you've skipped everything else and come straight here then you are a person after my own heart. Straight to the Taking Action section!

I will repeat a few of the lessons from the previous chapters, but I do encourage you to go back through to get more in-depth knowledge about what you need to do at each stage. If you can have a few things in place before you start, you can speed the process along:

- Eye-catching square image sized at 1080 x 1080 pixels. You can also have an image at a 4:5 ratio which would be 1080 pixels by 1350 pixels or oblong at 1200 x 628 pixels if you prefer

- Demographics and Keywords that you want to use for the targeting
- An idea of your budget that you want to use to start

Do you want to know the real secret to creating a high-converting ad? It's split-testing! You probably won't create a high-converting ad with your very first ad. But you can create a very good ad and then test again to get better and better.

Let's walk through the steps of creating your first ad. Just know that you may have to go through this process a couple of times with new ads before you get the results you want.

In the hour or less estimate, I mention spending **15 minutes on creating the Campaign, Ad Set, and Ad**. You've already done a lot of work in doing the research, creating the image, and writing the ad so this process will go quickly.

FACEBOOK TRAFFIC AD

A more powerful ad type can be the **Conversion ad**, but that requires a little more set up with the Facebook Pixel. You can learn more about setting up a Conversion ad in the Advanced Topics section of this book. I also cover this topic in depth in my Facebook Advertising Secrets course at https://fbadvertisingsecrets.com/opennow.

Facebook can be a great way to drive highly targeted traffic to your website at a great cost per click. To start you on the path to creating an ad and keep things simple, we will start with a Traffic Objective in this example.

STEP 1 - GO TO THE FACEBOOK ADS MANAGER AND START THE ADS CREATION PROCESS

Log into Facebook and select "create ads" or "manage ads" menu option. If you've never done an ad before, you may not see the "manage ad" section. Just go to "create ads." Or go directly to https://www.facebook.com/adsmanager/creation. If you have to do to the Manage Ads selection, you may then have to select the green Create button to start the ads creation process.

STEP 2 - CHOOSE THE TRAFFIC OBJECTIVE AT THE CAMPAIGN LEVEL AND NAME YOUR CAMPAIGN

You have a lot of choices here for objectives. But in this example, you will drive traffic off of Facebook to a website or landing page where you want the traffic to go. It's important to have a campaign name so that you can know exactly what that campaign was about and search for that campaign later if needed. I typically keep the Objective as part of the campaign name.

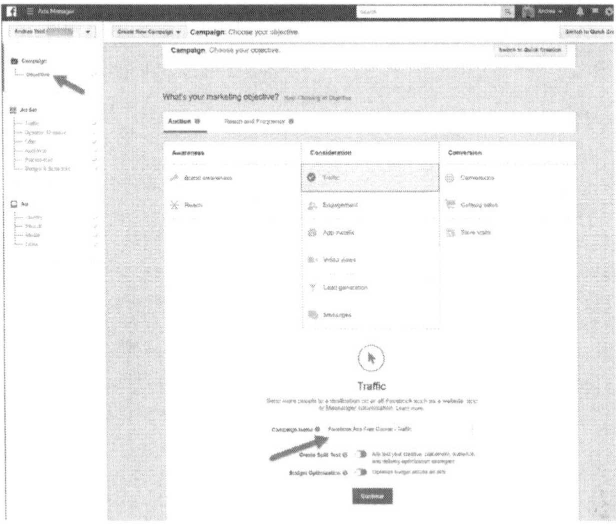

In this example, I am advertising my free Facebook Ads mini-course, so I give the Campaign a descriptive name but keep the Objective for the Ad in the Campaign name. Click the blue Continue button to move to the Ad Set level.

STEP 3 - NAME YOUR AD SET AND SELECT THE TARGETING FOR THE AD

At the top of the screen you will see a place to name the Ad Set which is going to make a difference when you look at the Facebook Reports. My naming convention for the Ad Set level is [Goal of the campaign] - [Objective] – [Demographics] - [Placement, if unique] -– [Ad features, if just one ad].

For this ad, I name the Ad Set "Facebook Ads Free Course - Traffic - US 35-55 W Social Media Examiner Hootsuite - Blue image with book". Your naming conventions may be different and you may use more abbreviations. The important thing is that you know what it means.

You can skip some of the sections that may talk about Dynamic Creative and Offer and leave the default setting of "Website" as the place to which you will send traffic and move to the Audience section.

In the Audience Section, you will select the demographics and keywords you have researched from the Targeting Your Ad chapter in the previous section.

In this case, I choose women in the US, age range 35-55 who like Social Media Examiner OR Hootsuite.

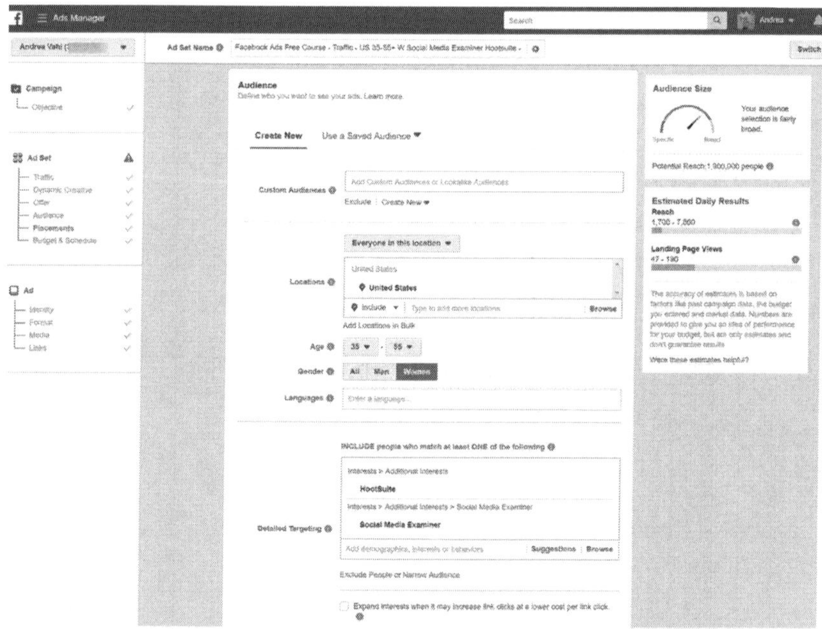

STEP 4 - EDIT PLACEMENTS

Make sure you edit your Placements. Facebook encourages you to select "Automatic Placements" and actually hides the Placements a little bit by making them less accessible. But not all placements are right for your ad. In my example, I don't want this ad to show on Instagram or the audience network or Messenger. So I leave those out and just run it on the Facebook News Feed on on the Right Column. The Audience Network is actually on sites OFF of Facebook so I rarely run the ads there. Uncheck any placements you don't want.

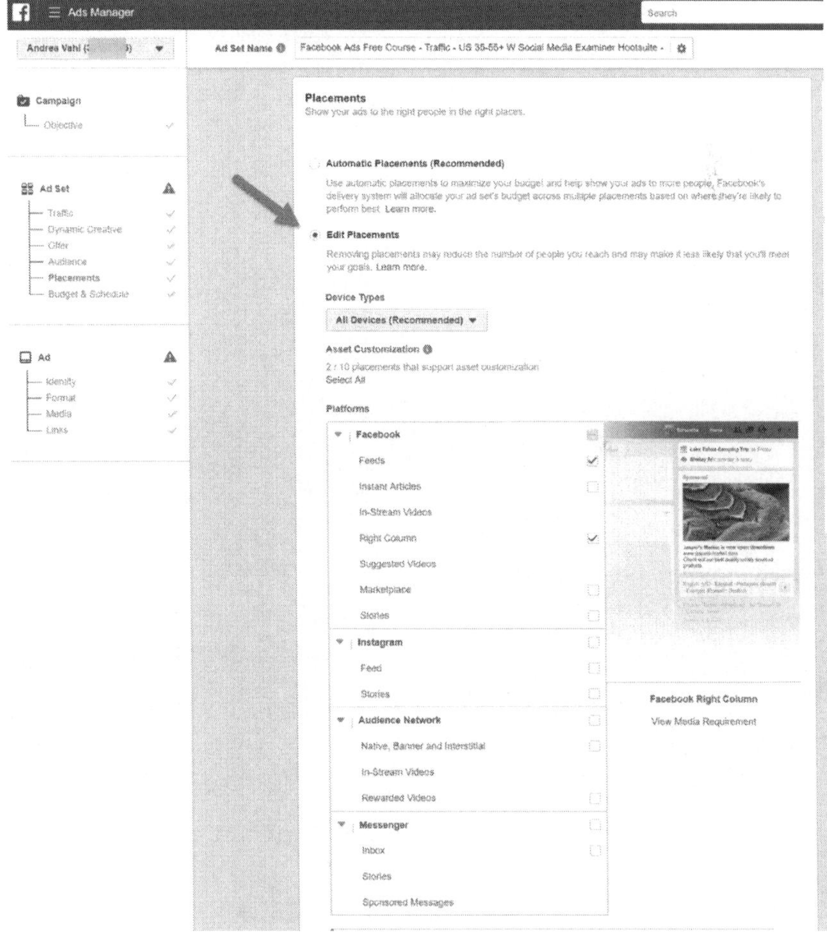

STEP 5 - SELECT BUDGET AND SCHEDULE

When you are starting out, you can keep much of the budgeting to the default settings. Choose your Daily Budget to be at least $5-10 and run the ad 3-5 days to test. You can extend the ad if it's doing well after the test period.

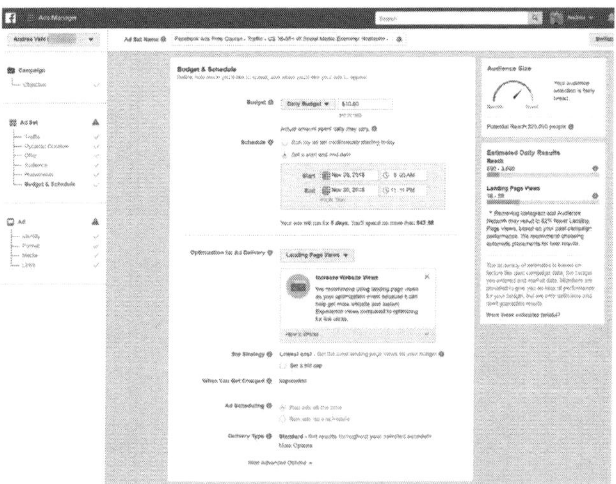

STEP 6 - CHOOSE THE AD NAME AND CHOOSE YOUR FACEBOOK PAGE

Name your Ad so that when you look at your Reports you will know which ad it was and you can read your reports easier. I typically will name the Ad Name the same as the Ad Set, but you might have a different convention. Choose your Facebook Page that will sponsor the ad from the dropdown menu in the Identity section.

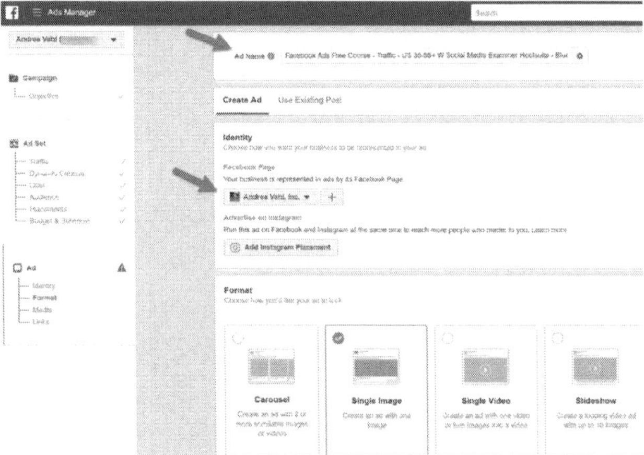

Occasionally, there is an odd thing that Facebook does if you are the Admin of several Facebook Pages. You may see only one or two Pages and there is a small arrow in the upper left of the drop-down menu. Click the back arrow to get to all of your Facebook Pages. Why oh why are you so crazy sometimes, Facebook??

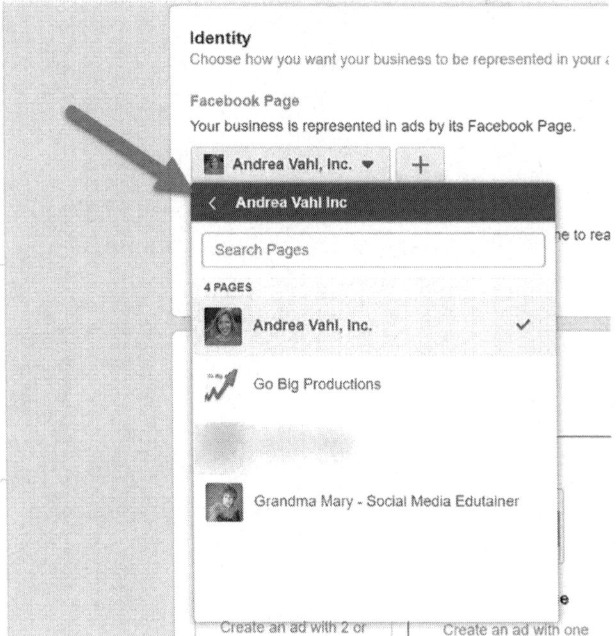

STEP 7 - UPLOAD YOUR EYE-CATCHING IMAGE

You created an eye-catching image in chapter 9 with a tool like Canva or PicMonkey. You can upload it with the "+" sign, but only upload one image at at time rather than multiple images or Facebook will create multiple ads for you. There can be advantages to trying multiple images but Facebook doesn't always optimize your budget over those different images properly. Creating a brand new ad to test a different image is a good idea when starting out.

Remember to keep the text on your ad to 20% maximum if possible (books and products don't count) so that Facebook doesn't stop your ad for too much text.

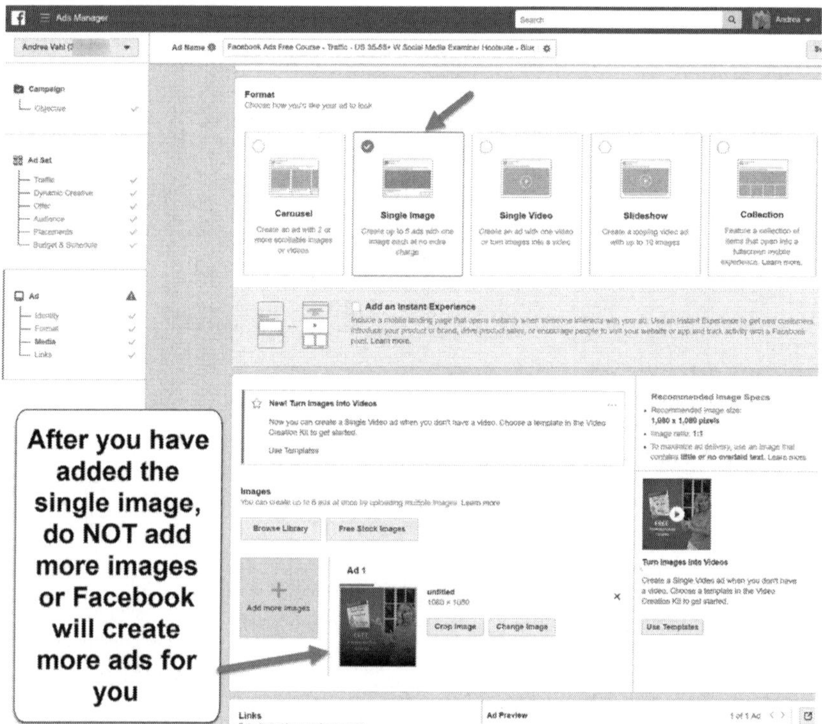

STEP 8 - WRITE THE TEXT OF YOUR FACEBOOK AD

Use the Problem, Agitate, Solution method that was covered in Chapter 6. Remember to avoid calling out specific traits or conditions that people have. Try to add in some social proof or highlight why you are an expert in this field. Focus on what makes your solution unique or desirable.

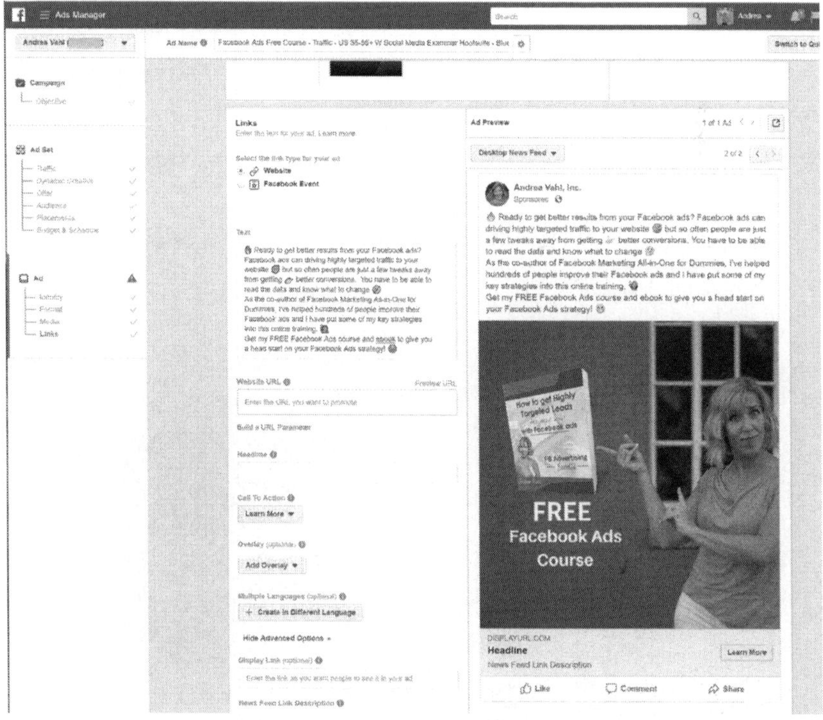

Emojis are working in ads and updates to capture attention. I use https://emojipedia.org/ to find different emojis.

There are different opinions on long copy (text) vs. short copy for enticing people to click over to your website. I typically see a little longer copy work better in general, but you can also text short text as well.

STEP 9 - ADD THE WEBSITE URL, HEADLINE AND CALL TO ACTION BUTTON FOR YOUR AD

When you add the Website URL, you may see that your Headline (the large text that appears under the image) is automatically added. This comes from the "meta data" that is on your website and may not be optimal for your Facebook Ad. The headline is the largest text in your ad (other than the text that might be on your image) so you want to make sure that is interesting to people.

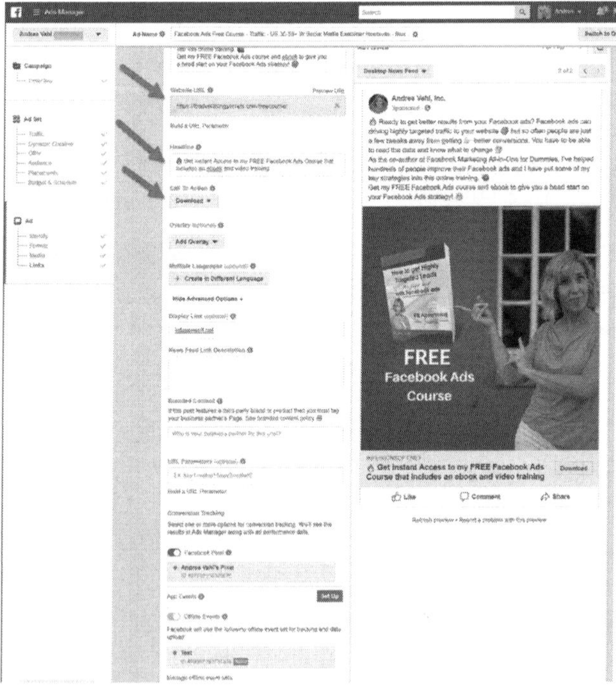

STEP 10 - REVIEW THE DIFFERENT LOOKS OF THE DIFFERENT PLACEMENTS OF THE AD TO MAKE SURE IT LOOKS GOOD ON DESKTOP AND MOBILE

At the top of the Ad Preview section, you can take a look at the drop down menu and see how your ad will appear in the Mobile feed or other placements you have chosen. Definitely look at this as the image and text may be cut off in different spots.

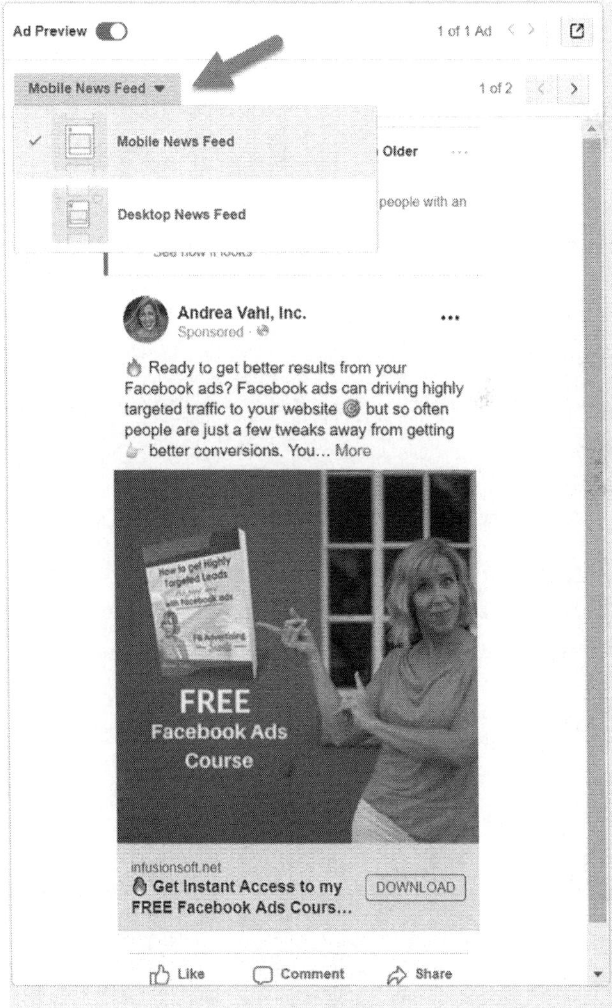

STEP 11 - MAKE SURE THE PIXEL IS CONNECTED AND ACTIVE IF YOU HAVE THAT INSTALLED

If you do have the Pixel activated, it should default to the "on" mode which will show with the green button under the Facebook Pixel heading.

STEP 12 - CONFIRM YOUR AD TO START RUNNING

Ignore the other sections like URL Parameters and Offline Events and "Request Manual Review" if that notification appears. The Ad will go through if there are no red warning symbols (if there are, you do need to get those fixed). It will go into the Review process, which can take anywhere from a couple minutes to 24 hours.

The URL Parameters are for tracking purposes and are a more advanced tactic. You can even ignore the News Feed Link Description because that section doesn't appear on many placements.

Be careful of adding any Display Link into your ad - Facebook will disapprove ads that don't have the same Display Link as where the actual link is sending the traffic. They should just remove that feature because it causes confusion!

If your ad is not approved, you will see a red "Not Approved" button and you will have to Edit the Ad to see why it isn't approved and make the necessary changes.

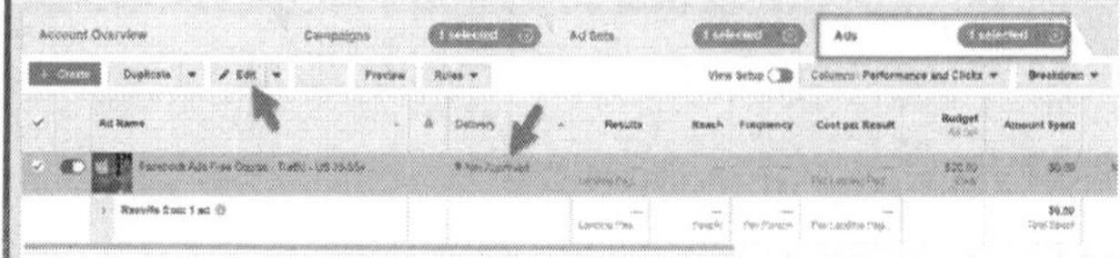

Your Ad will remain in the Review phase until Facebook decides that it does meet their advertising terms here: https://www.facebook.com/policies/ads/. Also see chapter 2 of this book for hints on language and images that don't work in Facebook Ads such as before and after images or using "you" in ads.

If you scheduled your ad for the future, you will see a "Scheduled" notification that will indicate the ad is approved and will run when you have set the time. If you need to edit the time the ads run, you must do that at the Ad Set level and then click on the pencil icon or the Edit button to edit the ad.

If you've scheduled your ad to start right away, then you will see an Active button under the Delivery column.

Congratulations! You did it!

BEST PRACTICES WHEN YOUR AD IS RUNNING

Facebook ads can be a bit finicky in terms of performance. There are also common mistakes that people make when they are just starting out that affect how well we can analyze the data we see in the Facebook Reports.

- **Don't edit your ad or targeting once it is running.** First of all, Facebook "resets" the momentum that the ad may have gotten so far so if it had been performing well, the ad may take some time to get to that performance level again. Secondly, editing the ad will be confusing in the reports because you won't remember exactly when you made those changes (you can find out, it just makes the reports less useful).

- **If you do need to make an adjustment on an ad, start a brand new one.** Minor adjustments to the schedule or the daily budget are fine but any major adjustments to targeting or text should be a brand new ad so that you can keep track of the stats individually.
- **Give the ad at least 1 day before stopping it.** I do suggest doing 3-4 days at least but sometimes you can see right out of the gate that the ad is a dud. But even that takes some time so let it run to get some momentum.
- **Increase the budget gradually if the ad is performing well.** Any major increases may cause the performance to start tanking. Typically, 10%-20% budget increases are okay. Make sure the performance stays on track for a day or two before increasing again.
- **Watch your reports each day.** You will learn more about what to watch for in the reporting section but you want to compare the right stats and watch the trends to see when the ad is underperforming or when you might want to add more budget.

As I mentioned, your first ad probably won't be your best ad. But now that you have one under your belt you can test more things and use better tactics to scale up! Yeehaw!

13

FACEBOOK ADS REPORTS

Your ad is up and running and it looks like things are happening but what do all those numbers mean? Is your ad doing okay? Which numbers really matter the most? Ugh, I should have paid more attention in math class!

You don't need to be a technical wizard to make sense of Facebook Ad Reports. You just need to set the reports up right and know what you just need to know where to look to see the trends of how your ad is doing.

FACEBOOK REPORTS OVERVIEW

Your Reports screen is the default view when you log into Facebook Ads Manager. If you navigate anywhere else in your Ads Manager, such as Audiences or Pixels, just go back to the Ads Manager selection from the hamburger menu in the upper left corner.

When you view the Reports, you may default to the Campaign view (the tabs across the top of the table) and Lifetime date range (in the upper right section). Or the view may default to whatever setting you were using most recently. It's important to know what you are looking at so that you are reading your reports correctly.

Let's dive in with a little tour of the report section first, and then I'll show you how to set up your reports in a meaningful way.

In the upper left, you have a search button so that you can search by campaign name and ad set name (which becomes more useful as you have more and more ads). That's why it's very important that you're naming your ads, ad sets, and campaigns well.

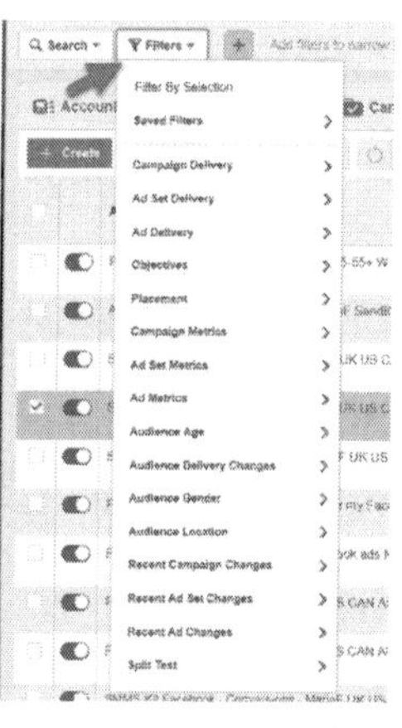

Then you have the Filter menu, which is really handy because you can kind of filter and compare different types of ads you might be running.

In the upper right is the date range selection. You can see there is no data in three of the Ad Sets showing in the image below because those Ad Sets weren't running during the month of November. The data shown is only for the date range you have selected. You can switch your date range to show last week or yesterday, for example, which allows you to see the trend with your stats.

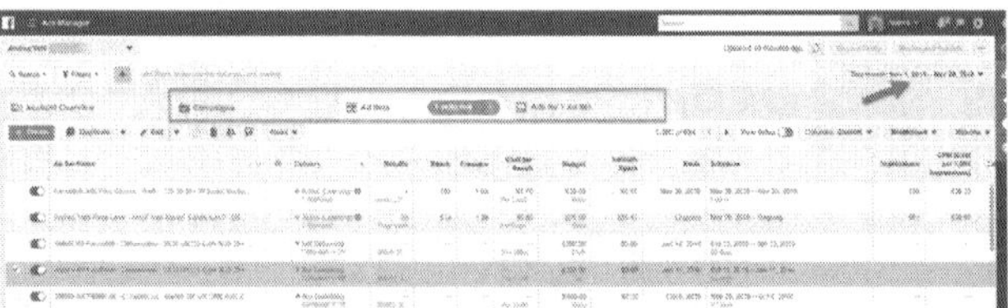

The tabs just above the table correspond to the levels of the Facebook Ad Campaign structure—Campaigns, Ad Sets, and Ads. You click on each tab to see the information at that level or edit an Ad Set or Ad for example. The Account Overview tab is also there, which gives you an overview of how much you've spent and what's been happening with your account.

Notice when you click on the Ads level tab, you see a thumbnail of the Ad images which can help you remember which ad was which but the naming conventions still are important. You can Preview or Edit the ad to get more information when you have one of the Ads selected.

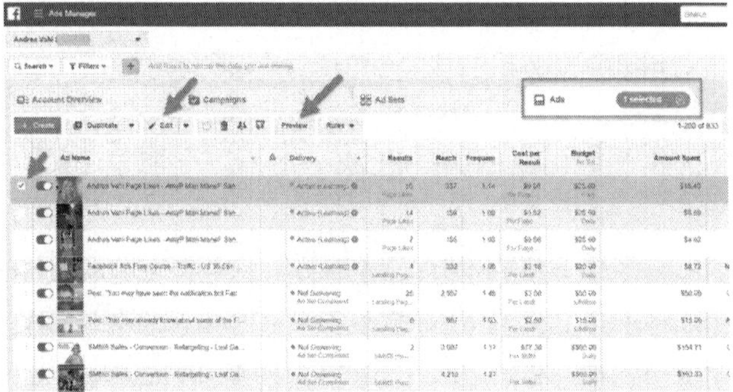

Then all the way to the right, there are some other icons that open up some additional information about the Ad, Ad Set, or Campaign you have selected. The graph icon at the top shows you a basic graph of performance (as shown in the image). The pencil icon is to make Edits and the clock icon shows you a history of changes. The bottom icon shows more details about performance at the Ad Set level.

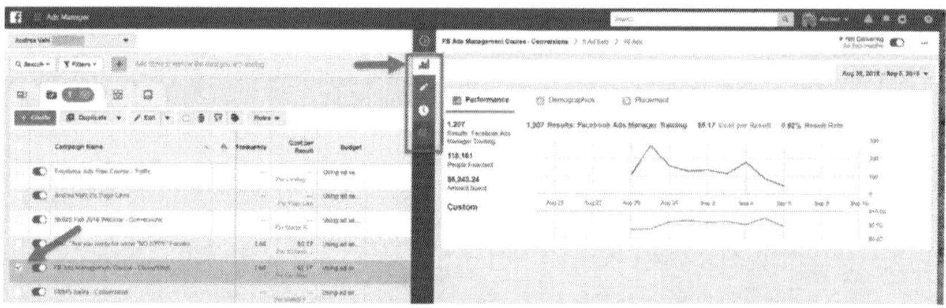

When you are at the Campaign or Ad Set level and you click on a hyper-linked Campaign or Ad Set name you are "drilling down" a level and filtering your view to only the Ad Set or Ads that are under that Campaign or Ad Set. In this example, I clicked on one Campaign and I can see just one Ad Set under that Campaign but I also have 3 Ads under that Ad Set.

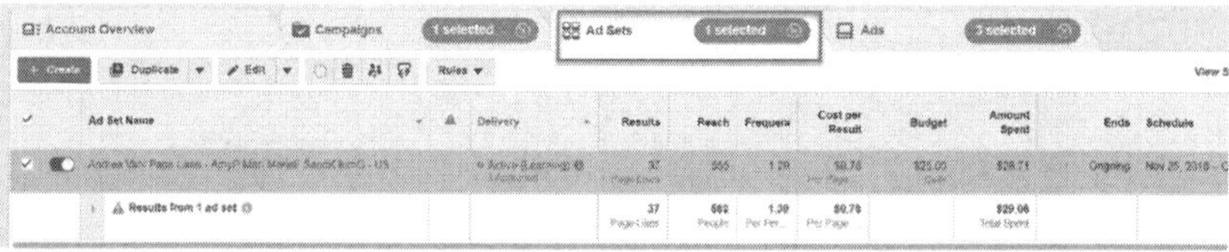

When I click on the Ad Set name, I then get to the next level where it breaks out the data from each of the Ads individually. It's important to know which level you are looking at, because the data may not accurately reflect what's going on with your ad campaign. For example, I can see that the one ad is giving me

$0.96 per Like but the other two ads are doing better at $0.62 per Like and $0.66 per Like. I normally don't run Like campaigns, but every once in awhile I like to test out how they do. At the Ad Set level, the data is combined to give me $0.78 per Like overall.

The columns you see are based on the preset report you choose, but you can also create your own report with just the stats you want to see. Facebook has a number of pre-built reports and columns. You can also customize your own reports and name them (more on this in just a bit).

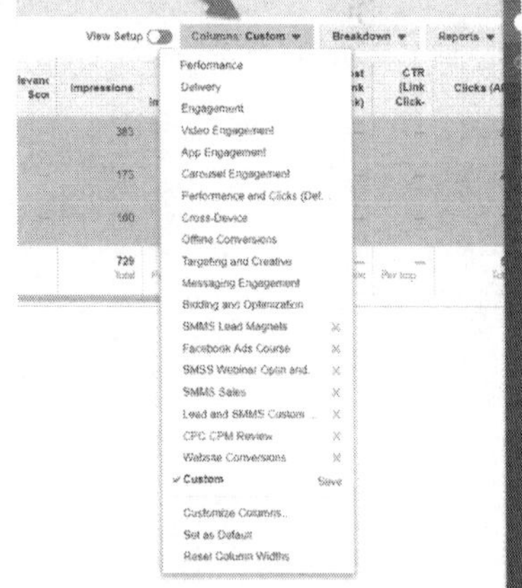

The Breakdown dropdown menu just to the right of the Columns menu is for viewing segments of your data in each Campaign, Ad Set or Ad. For example you can break out the Placement, or view your data by country or gender.

The Breakdown will help you in making decisions on what segments of your ad is doing well so that you can refine your testing and results.

There are more sections of the Reporting area but we don't need to know about every single button right away. I've covered the most important things you need to know right now.

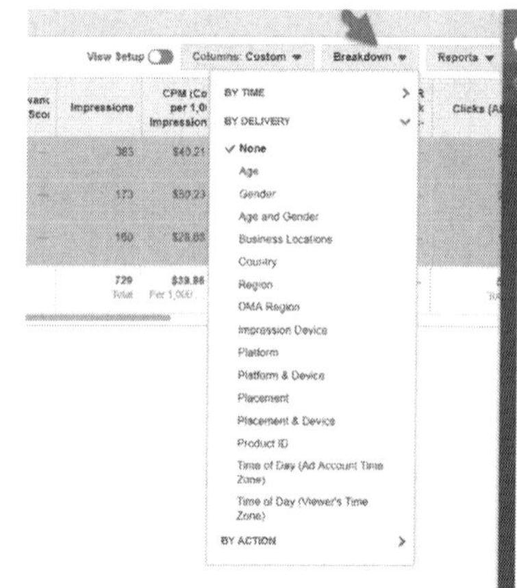

FACEBOOK AD REPORT SETTINGS

The best way to give you a head start on looking at your results is to talk about the custom reports that they have already pre-built for you. Facebook often defaults your view to the "Performance" report which doesn't give you enough information.

"Performance and Clicks" is the best default view for most Ads. You get information on the cost per link click and link click through rate (CTR). I often use that to start off my custom reports that I'm going to create. You can set this report as your Default view To set the Performance and Clicks report as your default view, follow these steps:

1. Click the Columns dropdown menu in your Ads Manager
2. Select Performance and Clicks, and your report should change to show you that pre-built report
3. Select Set as Default

Now you should see this view whenever you log into your Ads Manager. But sometimes it's a little flaky and still reverts back to a different view.

You can also customize your columns of your report to see more specific data that might be relevant to your campaign. When you click on "Customize Columns," you will see a popup box with all the possible data. It's a little overwhelming!

The good news is, you only need to focus on a few stats.

On the left side of the popup box, you can jump to the section of stats you might want to select. In the middle of the popup box, you can scroll through every possible stat with the scroll bar. Then on the right side you can remove columns or rearrange the columns (just drag and drop) of all the stats you have selected.

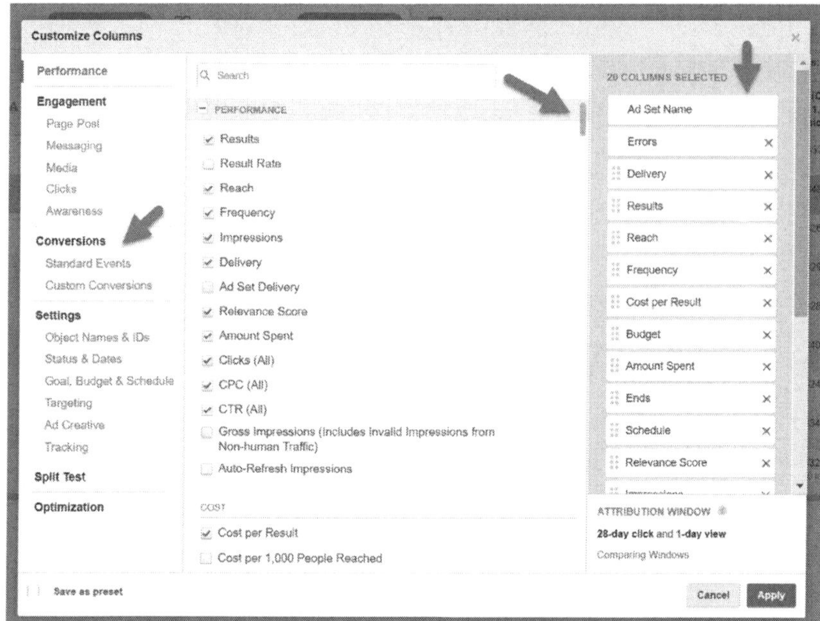

Typically the types of stats you should be adding into your reports are based on the Objective you have for your ad. Facebook does show the Objective in the "Results" column. What that means is you can't compare the ads against each other based on the Results column because those objectives are different.

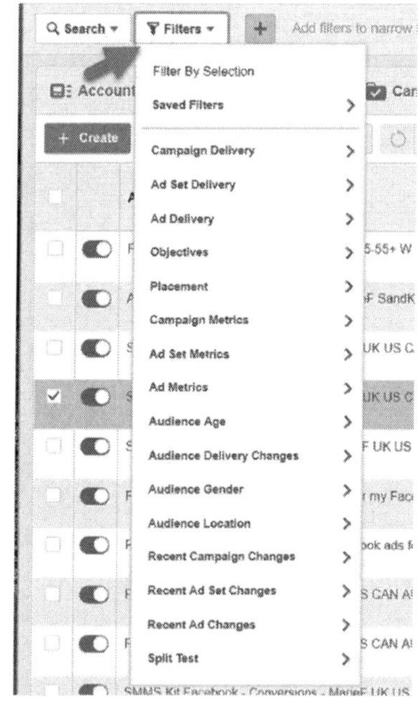

Notice that the Cost per Result column really changes based on what my Objective was in the ad. Some ads I was optimizing around Landing Page View, others was around 10-second video view, others were around Page Like, and then I had some optimized around a specific Conversion like SMMS Purchase, Starter Kit, Facebook Ads Manager Training. These are all Custom Conversions I set up. You will learn more about Custom Conversions in the Advanced Topics section.

Results	Reach	Frequency	Cost per Result
4 Landing Pag ...	365	1.07	$3.02 Per Landing ...
46 Page Likes	678	1.33	$0.75 Per Page Like
25 Starter Kit w...	9,138	1.11	$12.90 Per Starter K.
917 10-Second ...	8,610	1.66	$0.17 Per 10-Seco ...
1,207 Facebook A.	116,161	1.66	$5.17 Per Faceboo ...
25 SMMS Purc...	29,403	3.99	$98.12 Per SMMS P ...
177 Landing Pag ...	12,692	1.62	$1.78 Per Landing ...
36 Purchases	33,057	6.65	$78.97 Per Purchase
425 Facebook A...	29,024	1.65	$3.35 Per Faceboo...
138 10-Second ...	986	1.11	$0.06 Per 10-Seco...
229 Facebook A.	29,104	1.51	$6.98 Per Faceboo ...
17 Link Clicks	2,762	1.15	$2.20 Per Link Click
—	7,964	2.31	—

When you want to compare ads against each other, compare similar metrics. So look at the cost per link click or only compare ads that were optimized around the same objective.

FINDING YOUR BEST PERFORMING ADS

Your best performing ads are going to be based on what your key performance indicator is that you developed in the chapter on your Facebook Ad Strategy. You will also learn about some "typical" results later in this Taking Action section. But ultimately, you have to gauge your performance based on what is working for you.

Say my key performance indicator was to get the cheapest link clicks for each ad. I'm going to filter on only the ads that were optimized for Traffic and then click on the Cost per Result column to see which ones had the cheapest clicks. But if you also have the cost per link click column in your reports, you could sort by that column. If you haven't run a lot of ads, you may not have to filter your results.

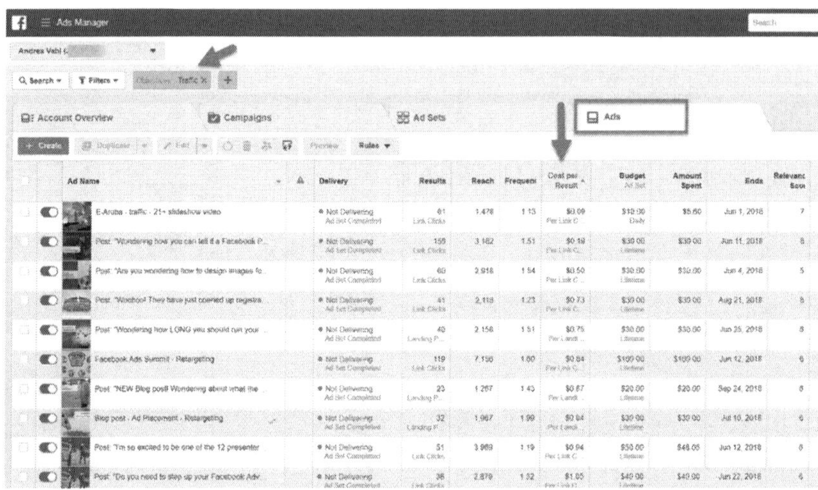

These ads are focused on different types of posts so it isn't a fair comparison. But the analysis process would be the same. The boosted posts (ads titled "Post") are optimized around traffic typically and can do very well for me to get people over to my website. The E-Aruba ad drove the cheapest cost per click, but that is a different target market of just people on Aruba when I was speaking there.

What I can learn from this analysis is what type of content does well to drive traffic. I can also see some posts that I might run again.

If I'm analyzing a set of ads that I have tested together with different targeting and different images, then I can make decisions on which one is giving me the best results and spend more money on the better performer. I'm cheap! I don't want to spend more than I have to!

In this example, I have several ads running under one campaign and I've tested different images and audiences. This is a Conversion ad that is optimized around the conversion of SMMS Checklist (which is a Custom Conversion I set up - more on this in the Advanced Topics section). I can sort by the ads that get the best cost per conversion and you can see that I stopped the ads that were underperforming with higher cost per conversion and kept the one running that was doing the best. Take that, Mark Zuckerberg!

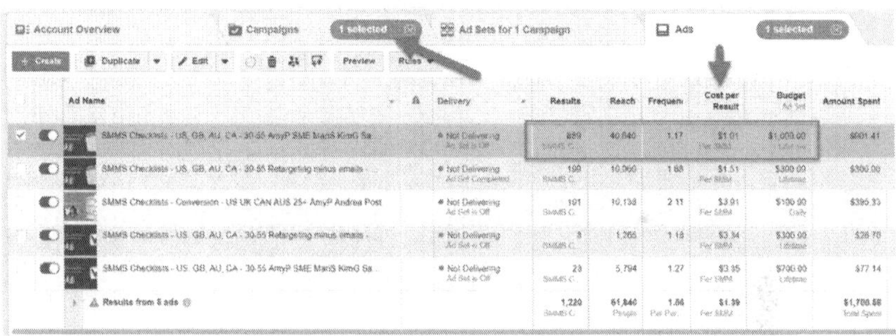

Also note that some of the data is only available at the certain levels of the report. For example, Relevance Score. This is Facebook's measure of how "relevant" your ad is to your target audience. The grade is from 1-10 with 10 being the best. If your ad had has a high Relevance Score, that's good and Facebook may give you better results. But I don't want you to live and die by the Relevance Score, because some ads in some markets are never going to get a great result. The Relevance Score is just a grade and it's based on the Click Thru Rate (good CTR means that people are finding it interesting) and other factors.

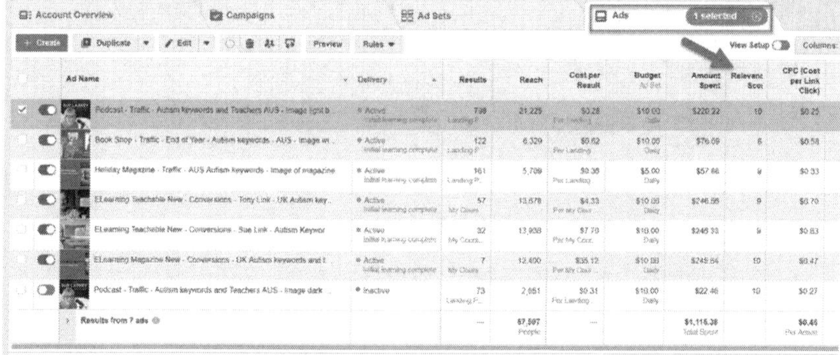

The more important thing is to focus on the metrics that are important to YOU. Getting a bad grade on an ad is bringing back my trauma from English class, so don't sweat it!

In the next chapter on split testing, you'll learn more about creating multiple ads and the best way to test different things so you'll need these skills on analyzing your ads when you do that!

14

BASICS OF SPLIT TESTING

What is split testing? What do we actually mean? It sounds hard, but it's actually a very simple process. But there are some different definitions and ideas around split testing.

What I'm talking about with split testing is changing one thing at a time and keeping all other variables the same. Then we know which variable led to the change in performance.

Split testing can also mean dividing up a group into two new groups and testing them separately to see which one does better. That kind of implies splitting off and kind of segmenting from a really large initial group.

Imagine if you created two totally different ads with different images, different text, and two totally different target audiences. One ad performed better than the other. That's great, you have an ad that did well. But you might not really know why, and you may not know the next thing to try.

When you come up with a systematic test plan for your Facebook ads, you can often get to the best performing ad more quickly. When you're first starting out, you may not know what demographics respond best. After you test your demographics, you can go back to that set of demographics over and over.

That's not to say that you don't want to occasionally try something new or see if maybe a new set of demographics might respond well. Facebook does change what kind of targeting capability it has. So you do want to kind of pay attention and try new things from time to time. For the most part, I'm running a lot of the same demographics over and over in a lot of my campaigns.

Facebook has a "Split Test" feature but I don't recommend it. It often requires a larger minimum budget than you might want to spend and they have other restrictions where you can't end an under-performing ad early. YUCK!

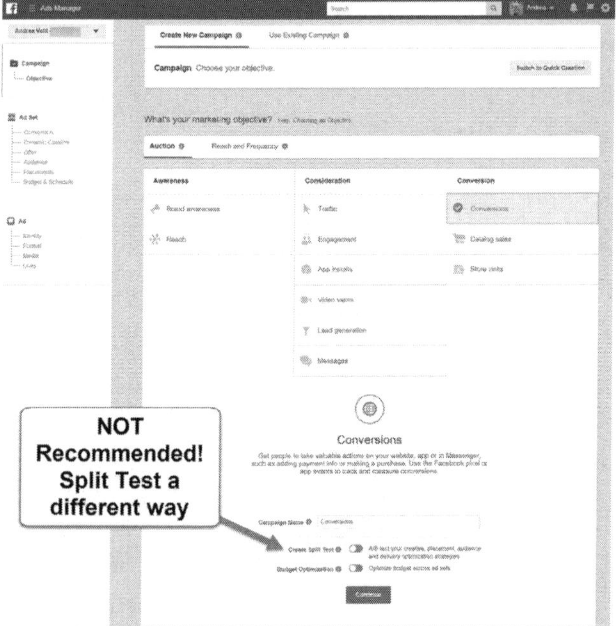

A better way to run split tests is to design them and set them up yourself. It's about the same amount of work and you have more control over your test.

In the hour or less estimate, I mention spending **10 minutes on split testing another ad**. Typically, you are going to test a different audience that you have researched but you may want to test a different image. This process should not take you too long to duplicate your ad at the Ad Set level.

FIRST STEP: TEST YOUR DEMOGRAPHICS

Your demographics is the first thing you want to test unless you really have that nailed down. Local audiences are an example where you aren't going to do TOO much testing. You know the area you want to target and maybe you have a few keywords that you choose on top of that. For local businesses, you can typically move straight to testing the creative aspects of the ad (the Second Step and Third Step in this chapter).

But if you did come up with several keywords you want to test in the Targeting your Ad section of this book, then now is your opportunity to see which keywords work best. Facebook doesn't tell us which keywords are performing the best if we lump all the keywords into one ad so it's up to us to test the keywords individually (or use logical groups of keywords).

Split Testing Ads – Group your Keywords

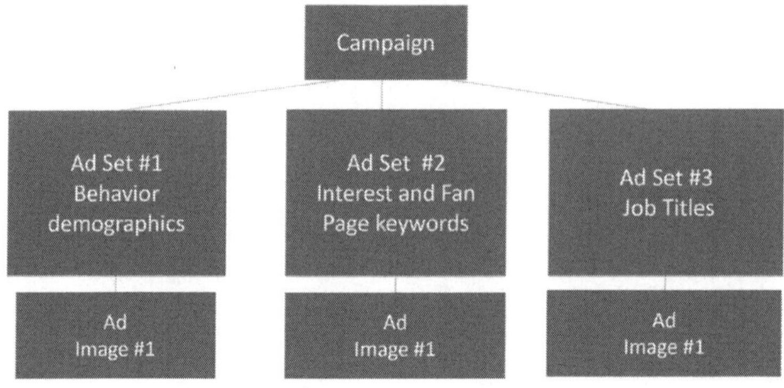

To review from the Strategy section, you might decide to group keywords a certain way and test them. You will create the same exact ad underneath each ad set to make sure those keywords are the only thing that is different about the test. *Note that there are some different ways to do split testing that are more advanced, but this is a good way to start for beginners.

For example, in my research I might come up with a list of keywords that would target people who would want to read a book in a certain genre like this:

- Mystery fiction
- Crime fiction
- Ebooks
- Ebook readers
- Agatha Christie
- P.D. James
- Sherlock Holmes
- Midsomer Murders
- Goodreads

- Amazon Kindle

Because some of these keywords are very large, I might do a few authors in one audience and then test Mystery fiction plus Goodreads in another.

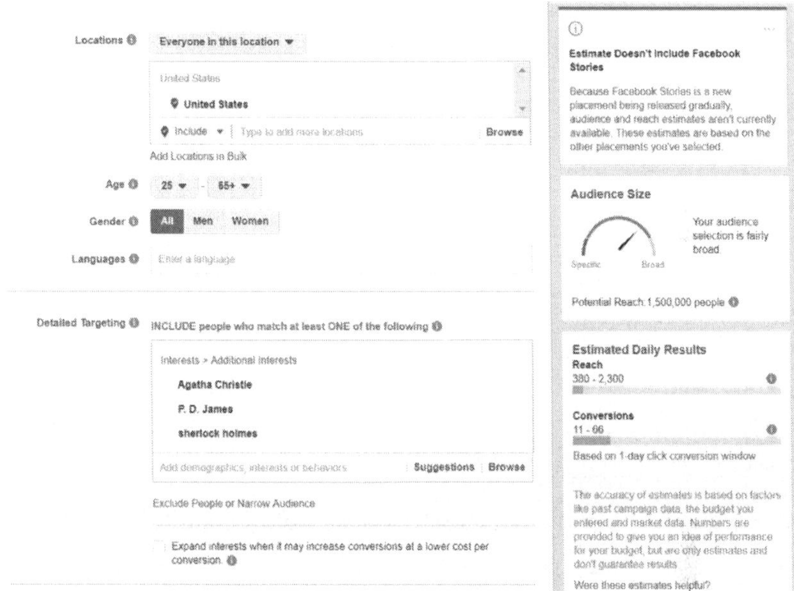

My other audience is larger, but that's okay.

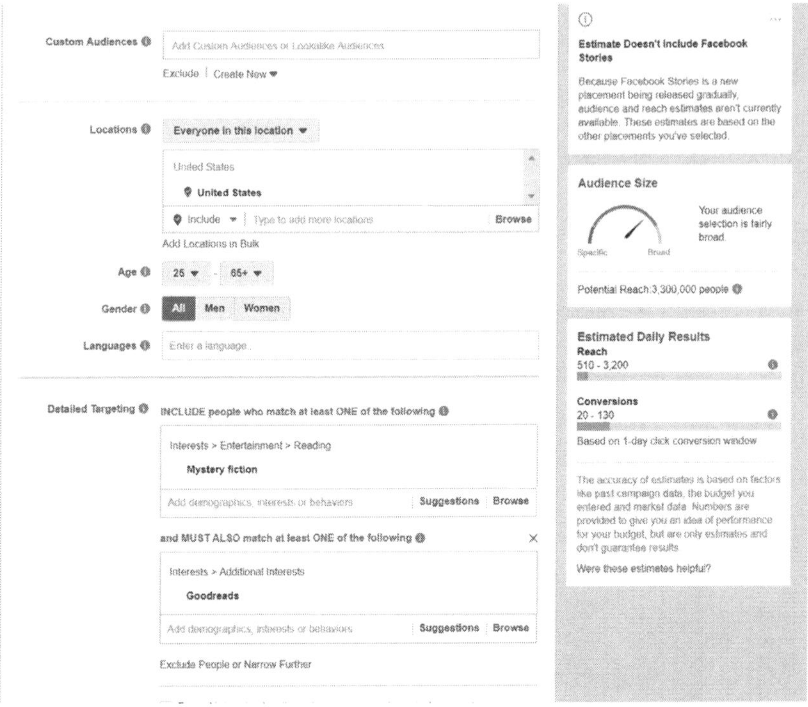

The ad and image will be exactly the same for each test so when you get our results, you know that the keywords were the thing that made the difference.

But what does split testing really look like in practice? The easiest way to accomplish a split test like this is to Duplicate the Ad Set, edit the targeting, and rename the Ad Set and Ad to reflect the differences.

CREATING A SPLIT TEST

First, you create an ad in the normal way (as shown in the Creating a High-Converting Ad chapter) and use one of the audiences you decided to test.

I typically suggest creating the split test at the ad set level because that is where the budget is set but you can create the test at any level.

Here are the steps to create a split test once you have your first ad finished.

1. Navigate to the Ad Set level in the Facebook Ads Manager. Check the box of the Ad Set you want to duplicate.

2. Select the Duplicate button that is just to the right of the green Create button.

3. A popup box appears and asks if you want to select the Original campaign, put the duplication into another Existing campaign, or create a New campaign. The box also may ask you if you want to do other things like add other placements. I typically turn those off and then select Duplicate.

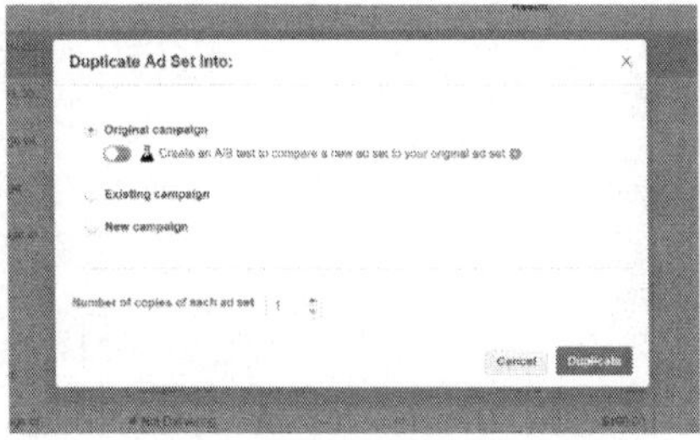

4. The new Ad Set will open to the right of your screen where you can change the Audience. Remember that you are now changing the targeting for the NEW ad that you created. I don't recommend editing the targeting for an existing ad that is running. The title of the Ad Set at the top will be whatever the previous Ad Set was with the word "- Copy" at the end. First, edit the Ad Set name with the new targeting or changes that you are going to use for this new ad. Then make those changes below. IF the only thing you are editing is the Ad itself, you can just keep everything as is in the targeting and change the name of the Ad Set to reflect the new information in the ad. **Click Publish when you have your changes made at the Ad Set level.**

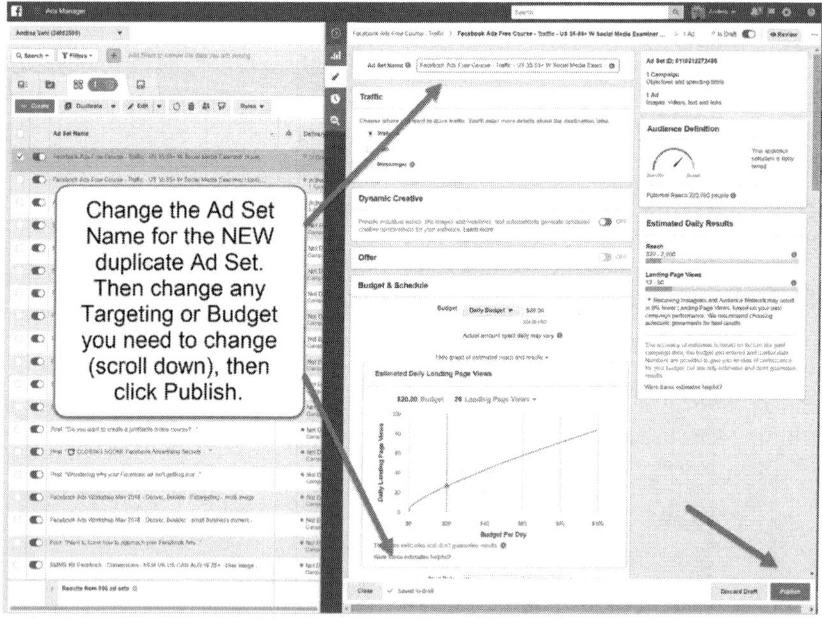

5. Your Ad Set will be in Review, but you want to make sure you make any changes needed at the Ad level such as re-naming the Ad so that your reports are clear. And if the only thing you wanted

to change was at the Ad level, you have to navigate there to make those changes. **Click on the name of the Ad Set to drill down to the Ad Level.**

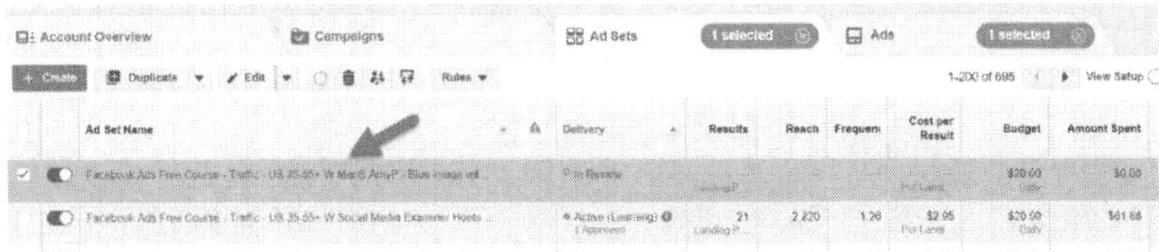

6. You see only the new Ad but it has the name of the "duplicated ad" that was under the other Ad Set. **Click Edit to edit that ad.**

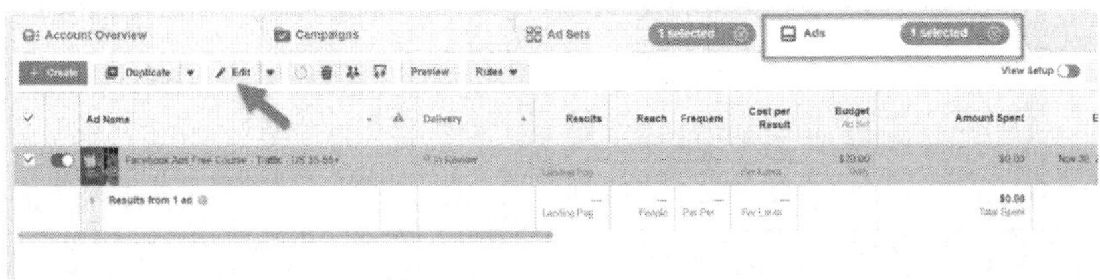

7. Remember, if you have changed the targeting at the Ad Set level, we don't want to change too many things at once. The only thing you would change in the editing of the ad is the name of the Ad so the report is clear. If you didn't change the targeting and wanted to change the Ad itself, then you can make those edits now.

8. When you click Edit, the ad will open up and you can make the edits to the Ad Name or the ad itself. **Click Publish to save those changes.**

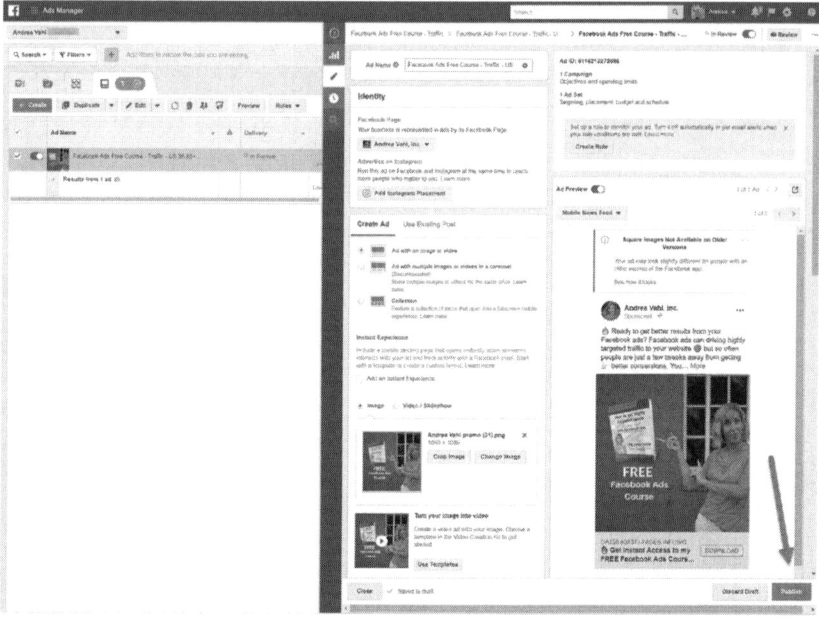

Now you are finished with creating your split test, and will be able to compare your results in the Reports area.

An advanced tip to be aware of is the fact that not all keywords will give you a totally "unique" audience. There may be people who like Yoga and Yoga Pants for example. There is a tool in the Facebook Ads Manager called "Audience Overlap" that can give you some insight to your audiences if you have them as "Saved Audiences." That is beyond the scope of "keeping things simple," but it's a tool you should be aware of once you get a little more advanced in your testing.

SECOND STEP: TEST IMAGES

Once you have the best performing audience, the next step is to test your images because those will make the next biggest difference to how well your ad performs.

You learned about this in our Creating Your Facebook Ad Image chapter, but here is a little more about how this works in practice.

SPLIT TESTING IMAGES:

1. Create several different types of images in Canva or whatever image tool you want. In this example I was advertising the https://thenonprofitacademy.com/. We tried several audiences first and then tries several different images.

2. Download the images from Canva.

3. Create the split test by duplicating at the Ad Set level as outlined earlier in the chapter. You can split test images at the Ad Level but

Facebook will not evenly split the budget for you and one ad may not get much budget.

4. Drill down to the Ad Level once you have Duplicated the Ad Set. Click the Edit button and the Ad will expand on the right side.

5. Click Edit and the ad will appear on the right side. Select Change Image.

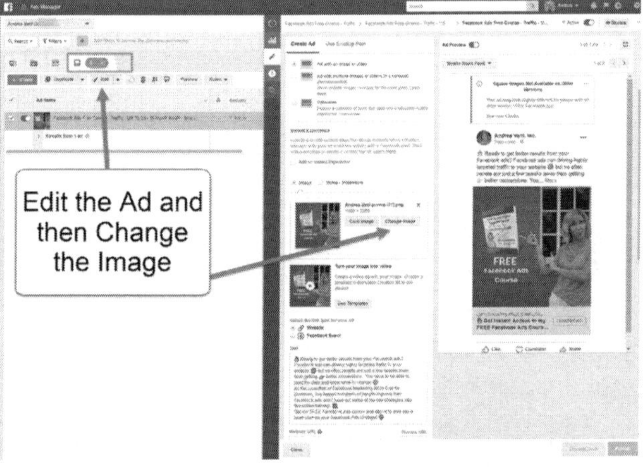

6. A popup box will appear, and you can upload the new image to your ad and click Publish.

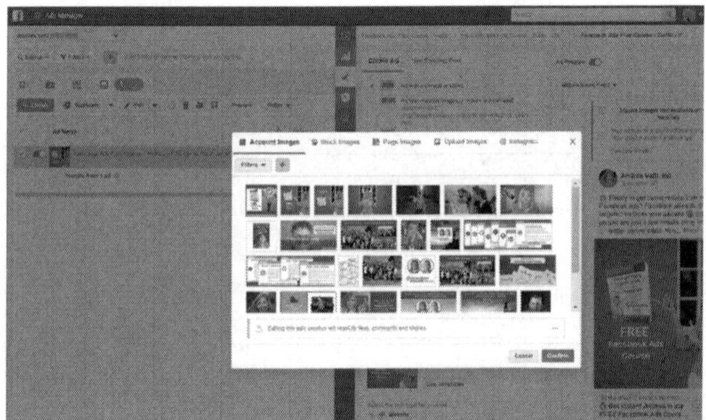

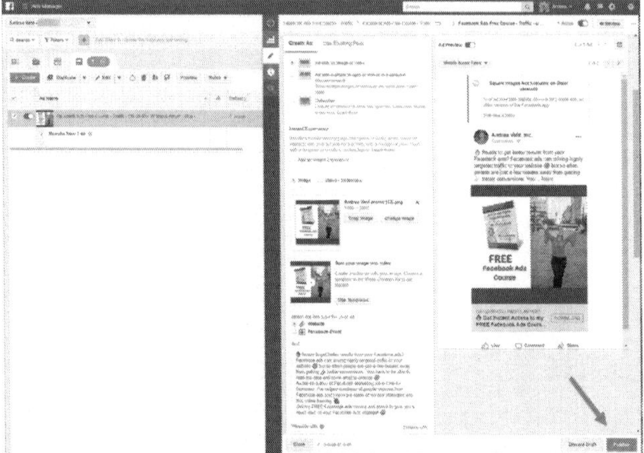

Now your job is to watch the reports and turn off any underperforming ads after a few days.

THIRD STEP: TEST AD TEXT

Choosing different text may be a little farther down the priority list but ad text still can make a big difference. New text can really refresh a tired ad campaign and can appeal to an audience in a different way. Again, the variations can be huge so I would focus on really changing the first section or headline of your ad as the more prominent change. You don't need to think about varying every sentence and testing them individually. Who has that kind of test budget?

Once you have your best performing demographic and a good image, you may try a few different text variations such as:

- Longer vs. shorter text
- A different headline
- Emojis in the text vs no emojis

- A different emphasis on what you are talking about in the text (different pain point)

Unfortunately there is no one-size-fits-all recommendation, such as 42 words with 3 emojis in each line works best. Different niches respond differently and you know your audience best.

REVIEW REPORTS

Reviewing your Reports when you split test is the same as covered in the Reporting section. You will be looking at the level that you split test your ads ad - typically the Ad Set level, but you could also be looking at the Ad level. You can see the thumbnail of the ads and then be reminded of which ad was which.

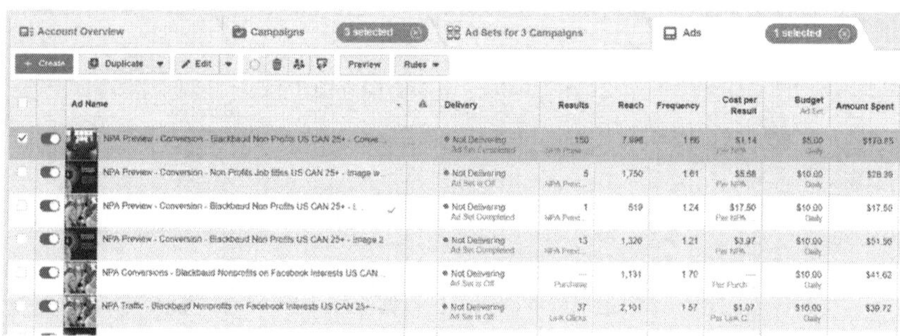

In this example from the Nonprofit Academy, we can see the first image on this report significantly outperformed the other images, giving $1.14 per conversion. That was actually not the image I thought would do well. So I guess wrong all the time! That's why you need to test.

Once you start testing, the challenge is to know where to stop. You could test every little nuance and not see significant results. Put a test plan in place based on how much you are able to spend for the testing phase.

For example, some clients I work with only have a total ads budget of $1000, so we don't want to spend more than $200 on the testing phase. If we are testing at $50/ad over 4 days, then we can only test 4 different ads. If that were the case, I would test 2-3 different audiences and test 2-3 different images depending on the available keywords.

Here is a visual example of how a split test might go. You test 2 different audiences in Phase 1 with the same ad under each Ad Set. Then you find that Ad Set 1 has the best performing demographic. The second phase you might test 2 new images (since you already have the results from the first image). So that is testing 4 different variations at $50 each for a total test budget of $200. Now when your test phase is done, you have the best performing demographic and the best performing image. You can continue to run that ad for the remaining budget.

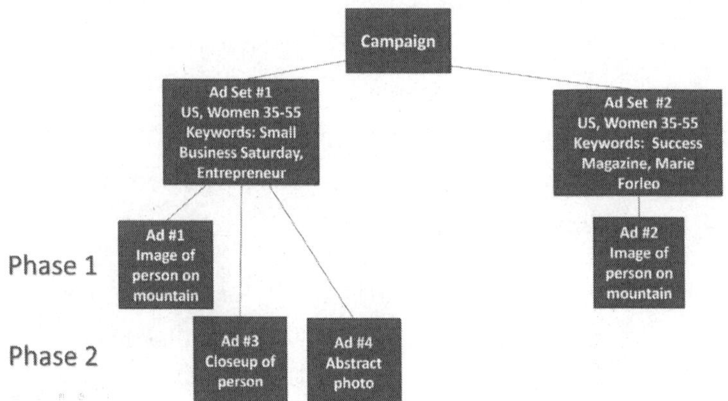

With split testing, your goal is to make educated guesses as to what will work best and then systematically test your ads. When you continue to test you, will get better and better at knowing what is going to work for your audience and continue to improve your results!

GREAT TIP FROM DENNIS YU OF BLITZMETRICS

> "The biggest Facebook ads mistake I see beginners make is they are too eager to 'turn knobs' instead of letting the algorithm do the work.
>
> For example, most beginners go nuts creating a ton of ad sets, each one with only a few dollars of budget. They are eager to test out many targeting options, but end up having so many ad sets that not one single ad set has enough traffic to yield 50 conversions per week. Thus, testing just a few ad sets at any point in time will let you learn quickly and give the algorithm enough room to find your winners.
>
> Facebook has been clear about the 50 conversions per ad set per week. And if you aren't hitting that, which the system needs to be able to optimize, you can choose 'add to cart,' lead, or whatever is one step up in the funnel as a proxy for conversion. You may have to also trim the number of ad sets you have, temporarily raise the budget, and try stronger creative.
>
> The other type of knob turning mistake is choosing the wrong business objective. Facebook has chided us many times for choosing the link click (website visit) objective instead of the website conversion or lead objective. If you choose clicks, the

algorithm will find the people within your audience that are "clicky users"— people who click all day for whatever reason, but don't buy. Then advertisers blame Facebook for poor conversion rates, when really the problem was in goal selection. Similarly, if you select 'video views' or 'engagement', the algorithm will seek those users within the overall target audience you specify. And those users will be quite different from those who buy.

Lastly, we see beginners making too many adjustments, like a gardener that pulls up his vegetable plants every day by the roots to inspect growth. Facebook isn't saying to be afraid of making budget and bid changes. But rather, don't be making bid and budget changes daily, since that resets the learning cycle. It doesn't reset the ad rank, which is the history of that ad or power in the auction. If you change the creative or targeting, that does reset the ad rank, so it's effectively a new ad."

Dennis Yu is the CEO of Blitzmetrics, an agency and also training company at https://blitzmetrics.com/. He's also a crazy-smart and super nice guy.

15

TYPICAL RESULTS

Now that you have your ads up and running with some split testing, how do you know you are getting the best results? What are the typical results that you should be expecting? And when should you turn an ad off?

Maybe you've heard people talk about getting Page Likes for 2 cents or new Leads for 10 cents a piece on Facebook. I'm here to bring you back to reality. While those numbers happen in certain industries with certain conditions, those results are NOT typical—and a little pie-in-the-sky for most businesses.

I recently heard something that made me very angry. A student of mine shared that her client got upset because she was expecting 1000 signups for a free course with a $200 Facebook Ads budget. And that included the "testing" phase of the project. That equates to $0.20/signup, which is ridiculous. It could happen, but I’ve never seen it myself. Even for something free.

In this chapter, I'll share some of the Facebook advertising campaign results that I've seen based on working with hundreds of different clients. You'll also see some industry benchmarks gathered by AdEspresso.

GENERAL BENCHMARKS FOR FACEBOOK ADS

I don't pretend to have access to vast amounts of data on every industry but I have had clients that are spending $1000+/day on Facebook Ads, and others that are spending $25/day. I've worked with people in all different types of industries: B2B, B2C, local, nonprofit, online products, events, schools, and more.

I like general benchmarks for some ballpark numbers, but what's important is to know your OWN numbers and do lots of testing. AdEspresso has great data in their blog post and report (https://adespresso.com/blog/facebook-ads-cost/) which I highly recommend you check out. They update this post every year with new data.

Here are a few of my favorite charts from that report, shared with permission. First CPC can vary widely by country (cost per link click in this graph). And it can also can depend on what type of ad you might be running. In this example, they limited it to campaigns with Traffic or Conversions as the objective.

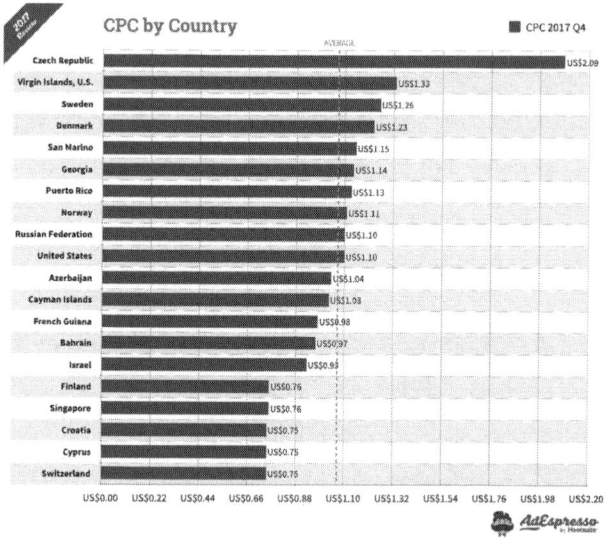

The costs can also vary quite a bit by Placement. Notice that the Audience Network is much lower for Link Click cost, but I always uncheck that placement because I haven't seen good conversions there personally.

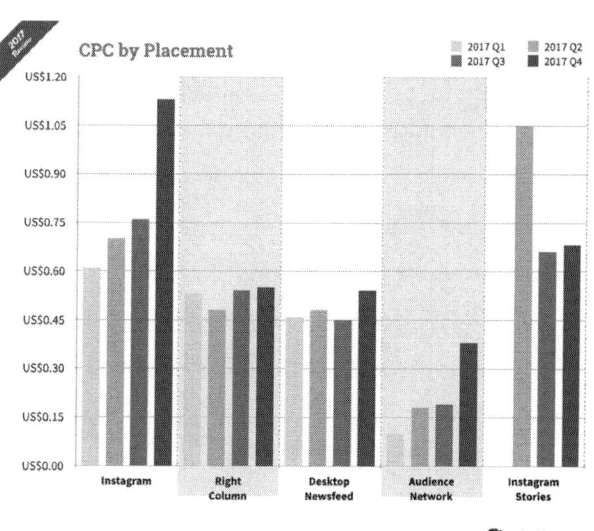

You can see here that Instagram has some of the highest cost per link click cost, which resonates with what I've seen before. Even for some businesses that have a good Instagram following, the link click cost can still be high. But you should test your own ad placement if you think that Instagram will be a good venue for you.

One of the other observations from AdEspresso is that CPC and conversion cost are higher in the 4th quarter of the year in general. There is more competition with the holiday promotions and special offers that people are making. When there is so much competition for ad space, you might find that your ads aren't going through all the possible budget—which happens in a crowded market.

RESULTS DEPEND ON THE NICHE, TARGETING, AND TYPE OF AD

While these benchmarks are a good place to start, different niches can see wildly different results. Sites like Wordstream, Salesforce, and Nanigans also have Facebook Ad benchmarks based on industry.

Clearly a dentist targeting a local area with a message of "come in to get your teeth cleaned" is not quite as exciting as a someone selling dog toys online with pictures of cute puppies. Not that a dentist can't be successful on Facebook—I've seen plenty of dentists doing great things on Facebook and even helped some with ads.

But I've put together my own set of guidelines based on my years of working with different industries. I have a range that I usually see for MOST niches I've worked with. Some are outside these ranges depending on the niche and what they are promoting.

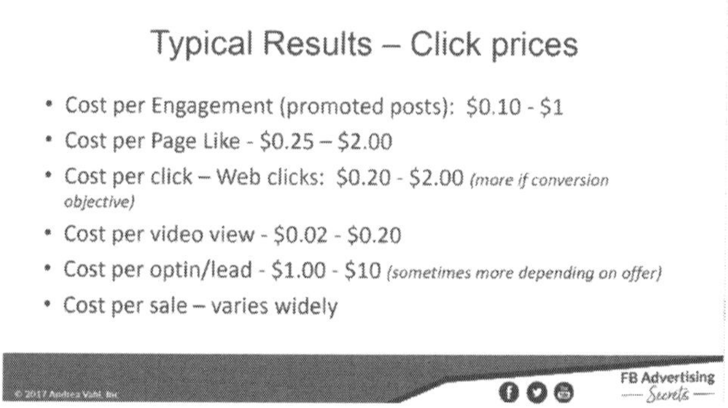

Typical Results – Click prices

- Cost per Engagement (promoted posts): $0.10 - $1
- Cost per Page Like - $0.25 – $2.00
- Cost per click – Web clicks: $0.20 - $2.00 *(more if conversion objective)*
- Cost per video view - $0.02 - $0.20
- Cost per optin/lead - $1.00 - $10 *(sometimes more depending on offer)*
- Cost per sale – varies widely

FB Advertising Secrets

Here are a few notes about each of these options:

- Cost per Engagement (boosted posts): $0.10 - $1 - I'm typically seeing better cost per engagement when something is very interesting to begin with and getting a lot of shares. So promote your most interesting posts that also further your goals. If you are promoting a more "salesy" post, it will typically be more expensive. It also depends on what type of audience you are choosing here - The Fans-only option is often less expensive since they are familiar with you.
- Cost per Page Like - $0.25 – $2 - Again, this can depend on your industry. B2B can be more challenging since the targeting can be harder.
- Cost per click -Web clicks: $0.20 - $2.00 - This depends on the topic and the targeting.
- Cost per video view - $0.02 - $0.20 - Video views are very inexpensive, but you have to make sure they are part of your larger strategy.

- Cost per optin/lead - $0.50 - $10 (sometimes more, depending on offer)
- Cost per sale – Varies widely

These results will also depend on how your are optimizing your ads. I see much higher cost per link click when I'm optimizing for Conversions.

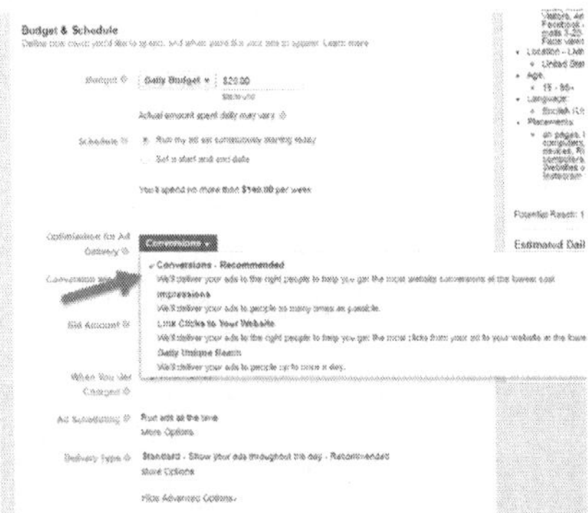

I typically see better conversions when I optimize for conversions rather than link clicks. Facebook tracks the people who are most likely to opt in to your offer or buy something and then shows your ad more often to those people (they are also within the targeting that you have specified).

Typically, if something is outside these ranges given here then it might be time to examine your targeting. Also try to look at different ways to optimize the ad,and do more split testing. It could just be a function of how your niche and targeting always perform.

For example, I have a client that routinely has optin rates that are in the $25-50/optin range. But that is worth it for them because they have a high ticket item and are able to get the return on their investment. Make sure you are calculating your own personal costs to determine how much you can spend on a lead.

Another stat I like to watch to make sure my ads are interesting to my target market is the Click Thru Rate. CTR is the ratio of people who clicked on the ad over the number of people who saw it. It's not always critical that you have a high CTR, because truly you just care about the main goal of the ad (like driving traffic, getting optins) and whether you are achieving that goal. But an ad with a higher CTR is typically "rewarded" by Facebook with lower click prices.

Good CTR is typically anything over 1% for the News Feed Placement, and if you are getting over 2% that is very good!

Wordstream has data on average CTR by industry here: https://www.wordstream.com/blog/ws/2017/02/28/facebook-advertising-benchmarks

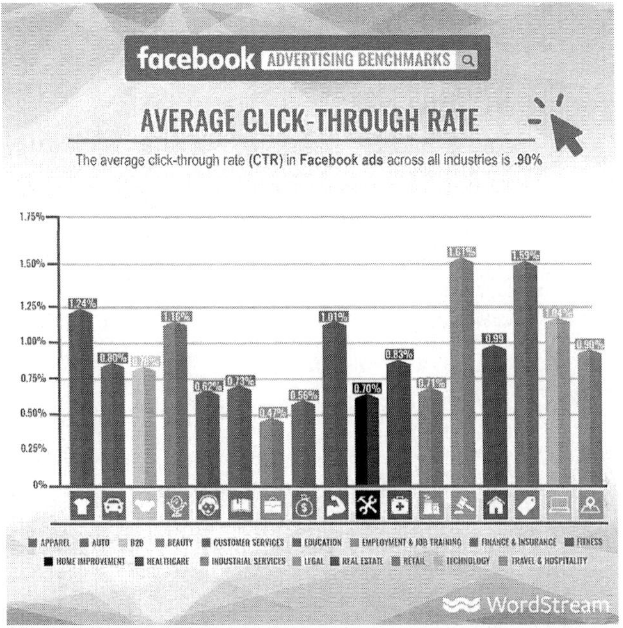

Sidebar ads get much lower click thru, and people often wonder about running them at all. But I do often keep the sidebar placement because it doesn't use much of the Ad budget and I often get good results with my sidebar ads. Sidebar ads are only visible on Facebook Desktop and more people are accessing Facebook with mobile devices these days.

ESTIMATING YOUR RESULTS FOR FACEBOOK ADS

One thing that frustrates me with people's expectations of Facebook ads is that they expect them to outperform any other type of marketing in the history of marketing. Then they get mad when they don't.

If you are going to track Facebook ad ROI closely, hopefully you are tracking the ROI of ALL of your marketing efforts so you know which tactics work best.

A couple of things I recommend to estimate and track your results:

- **Know what your conversion rate is in general for the sites to which you are sending traffic.** What is your offer currently converting at with regular traffic? Sometimes you may not know that if your offer is new. Do a few quick tests to determine a baseline. That may shift when you start sending more traffic there but it's a place to start!
- **Figure out what return you need for your marketing.** If you are selling a $3 book on Amazon, you shouldn't spend $4 on ads to get a sale. But growing your email list with targeted buyers who will buy your other books may be a good longer term strategy.
- **Make sure you have tracking in place to specifically track Facebook Ad conversions.** That way you will know exactly which Facebook Ads are working for you. You do this by getting the Facebook Pixel installed and setting up a conversion tracking method (which you'll learn more about in the Advanced section)
- **Track conversions with Google Analytics and Goals.** Google Analytics is free to add to your website. You can track any conversion on your website (not just ones coming from Facebook) with Google Goals inside of Google Analytics. This will help back up your data you get from your Facebook Ad reports and also help you track your conversions from other traffic. You can learn more about Google Goals here: https://support.google.com/analytics/answer/1032415.

Estimating your Facebook Ad Spend is just about gathering some numbers and putting them into an equation. We need to know the conversion rate of your offer (or product), the website click cost you normally get with Facebook Ads (feel free to use something in the middle of the range), and the desired number of leads or sales.

(Conversion Rate) * (Website Click Cost) * (Desired number of leads) = Ad Spend

Example:

- Conversion rate of website = 10%
- Website Click cost = $0.50
- Desired number of leads = 100
- (0.10) * ($0.50) * (100) = $500

With this equation, there are a couple of things to keep in mind:

- I typically see better conversion rates when I'm sending targeted traffic from Facebook to my site compared to general traffic
- It is usually much more difficult to sell directly on Facebook than to offer something for free to get leads
- With the way Facebook optimizes for conversions, it's better to just plug in what your cost per conversion typically is rather than look at the cost per website click of a conversion ad

So in that case, I'm often getting between $1-2/conversion with my lead magnets.o that's straight math of $2/lead * 100 desired leads = $200 Ad spend.

HOW TO GET YOUR FACEBOOK ADS COSTS DOWN

I have a few key tips to bringing your Facebook Ad costs down:

1. **Offer something that your audience cares about as a lead magnet.** If you aren't getting good results with one lead magnet you may need to test a different offer. I've had clients that have used the exact same title and content for a webinar, then turned it into an ebook and more than doubled their optin rate.
2. **Split test your ads.** You learned about this in the last chapter but this is the best way to get your costs down—test different target demographics, different images, and different types of ads. Turn off the ads that are underperforming and only run the ads that get the best conversions.
3. **Target your warm audience.** Typically your warm audience (the people who already know you) are going to give you the best results. You can target your email subscribers, your website visitors, and your current Facebook Fans with ads. You might say that you don't want to target those people since they already see your messages. But they need reinforcement! How many times to you purchase something the instant you see it? More often than not, we are getting reminders. Not everyone opens their e-mail or reads every blog post you have. Obviously, you don't have to target your email subscribers if you are trying to grow your list but you can target all the people who have visited your website EXCEPT the people who have already signed up for your newsletter.

Facebook ads are powerful. And they are one of the lowest cost places to advertise online today. You can save so much of your marketing budget by only focusing your ads to the people who are your ideal client. When you measure your marketing efforts, you can make smarter choices about what channels to focus on and which activities to drop. But just make sure your expectations are grounded in reality!

16

CONVERSION ADS AND LEAD GENERATION ADS

Conversion Ads and Lead Generation ads are some of the most powerful types of ads you can run on Facebook. You may already be getting conversions or leads from the Traffic ads you are running. BUT when you run a Conversion Ad or Lead Generation Ad, Facebook optimizes the ad to get MORE conversions and leads. SWEET!

Many people are confused about the difference between a Lead Generation ad and a Conversion ad. I find that people often select the wrong objective and aren't sure why it's not working correctly.

A lot of people see "Lead Generation" and think, "Yes, that's what I want – more leads!" But that objective may not be what you think it is and the Conversion objective may be the choice you should really be making.

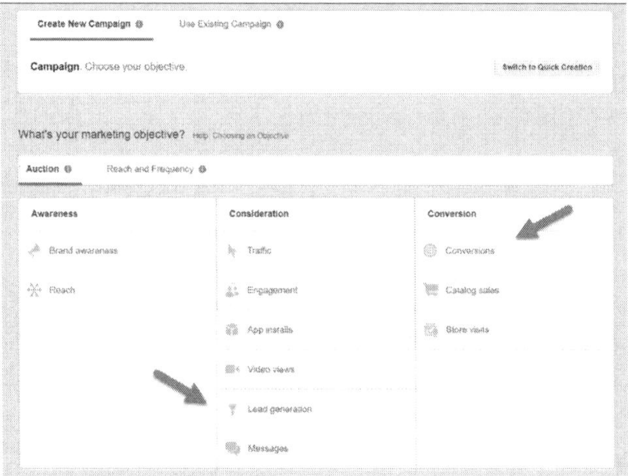

In this chapter, you will learn what the difference is between a Conversion Ad and a Lead Generation Ad, what you need to run these ads, and how to get started. Both of these types of ads are more involved, so I will not cover every step to use these ads but you will get a good sense of what it takes to get started. I cover these concepts much further in my online Facebook Advertising Secrets course at https://fbadvertisingsecrets.com/opennow.

THE MAIN DIFFERENCE BETWEEN A LEAD GENERATION AD AND A CONVERSION AD

The biggest difference is a **Lead Generation Ad happens all ON Facebook** and a **Conversion Ad you are sending the traffic OFF of Facebook** (to your website that has your own Facebook Pixel installed on it)

If you have a "landing page" or website that you want the traffic to go to, then you need to select the Conversion Ad and you should make sure you have the Facebook Pixel set up correctly. Earlier in the book, you created a traffic ad and sent the traffic from your ad to your website. If you have some type of optin or if you are selling a product or service on your site, you can use the Conversion ad instead to optimize around conversions.

If you don't have a landing page or website but want to collect leads, the Lead Generation ad is a perfect solution for you.

Here are some of the other differences between Lead Generation Ads and Conversion Ads.

FACEBOOK LEAD GENERATION AD	FACEBOOK CONVERSION AD
Gather Leads through a popup form ON Facebook	Gather Leads through an optin form on your website
NO website address or URL needed for this option	Direct traffic to the website or URL
Build a form to collect the data in Facebook	Form on your website typically comes from your email system
Form data goes into the Publishing Tools Section on your Facebook Page	Form data goes into your email system automatically
You can redirect someone to a website after they submit their form	You must redirect someone to another page on your website to register the conversion after they submit their form
Does not need the Facebook Pixel	Must use the Facebook Pixel
Facebook calculates the cost per lead based on when people submit their data in your form	Facebook calculates the cost per lead based on if they reach the Standard Event or Custom Conversion you specify in your Ad setup
Facebook pre-populates the form with the data that you ask for from the Facebook profile (can be easier for the user since they don't need to type their email address)	Person must manually type in their data into your form on your website.
You have to manually download the data to get it into your email system (or pay for a service to automate the process)	The data is automatically added to your email system from your website optin form

I typically prefer Conversion Ads to Lead Generation Ads because I already have an optin created on my website to gather leads and I like that the form on my website is already connected to my email system. The website can be more customized to give more information about the lead magnet that you are giving away. But a Lead Generation Ad can be a good way to gather leads if you don't have a form on your website.

EXAMPLE OF A LEAD GENERATION AD AND A CONVERSION AD

The best way to explain the differences between a Lead Generation Ad and a Conversion Ad is to show how they work. The ads themselves actually look exactly the same in the News Feed, but the flow is a little different.

This is a Lead Generation ad—there is actually no way to tell from looking at it that it's a Lead Generation Ad. You can only tell when you click on the Download button.

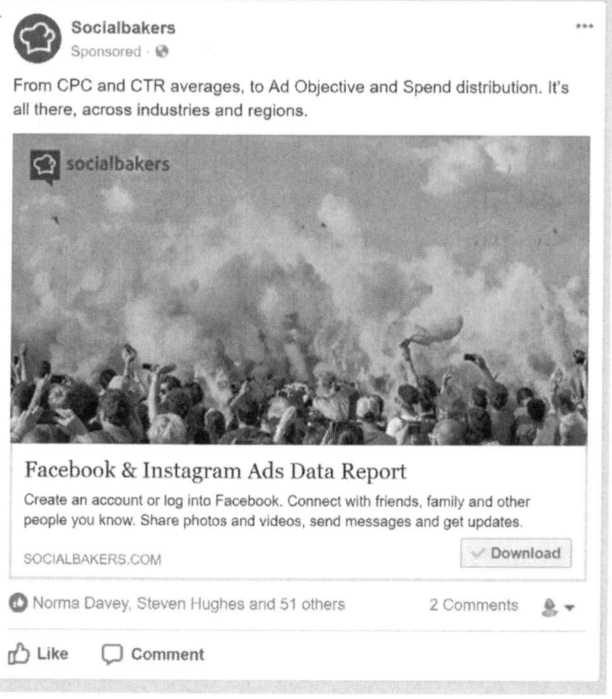

When you click the Download button, a popup box appears with more information about what you will get and also with your pre-filled information. You then have to confirm that you want to give the advertiser your information. You can "opt in" in 2 clicks without having to leave Facebook.

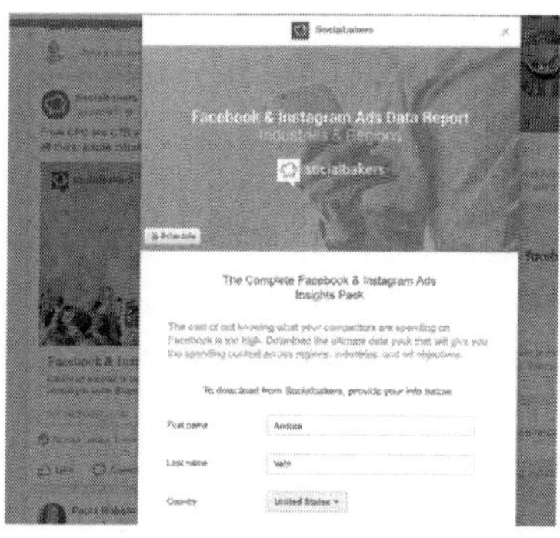

With a Lead Generation ad, you can "redirect" someone to a Thank You page after they confirm their information, so that they go right to the location on your website where you have the free thing you promised them.

When someone opts in to the Lead Generation form, you get their information (based on what you requested) in the Publishing Tools section on your Facebook Page. So if you don't redirect someone right away after opting in, you will have to email them the follow up information manually.

The Lead Generation ad is optimized to get more Leads. Facebook will show the ad first to people (within your targeting parameters) who are more likely to opt in to the Lead form.

Now compare the Lead Generation Ad to the flow of a Conversion Ad. You click the ad, and go to a website where you fill in your information and then get redirected to the Thank You Page where you deliver the free item. This redirect happens through your email system that you have set up such as MailChimp. The example shows a website built with the LeadPages tool that can also redirect people automatically.

This flow can be exactly the same as a Traffic ad where you send traffic to your website and then people can opt in. But the difference is that Facebook optimizes your ad to show it to the type of people who are more likely to convert. Facebook tracks all that we do and knows the type of people who optin in to Lead forms or who opt in on Conversion ads. Yes it's creepy, but it helps marketers!

WHAT YOU NEED TO RUN A CONVERSION AD

The Conversion Ad sends traffic to your website (or a website where you can add your own Facebook Ads Pixel) and then tracks the fact that someone takes another action on your website. A Conversion Ad can be tracking whether someone opts in to a free offer or whether someone purchases something as well as other actions someone takes on your website.

Here are some of the possibilities that you can track with Conversion Ads:

- Opt in to a free offer
- Purchase a product or service on your site
- Signs up for a webinar
- Adds something to the Cart but doesn't purchase (or does purchase - but you can retarget the people who don't purchase the product - so cool!)
- Completes a Contact form on your site
- Starts a free trial

Basically, anything that has another step on your website can be tracked with traffic that comes from your Facebook Ad. You just need to have the Facebook Pixel installed and then configure what you want to track.

You will be tracking these things from specific Facebook Ads only. The pixel doesn't track from individual Facebook Posts. But you will know exactly which ad is converting the best for you.

To be able to track conversions you need to have two things in place:

1. Your Facebook Pixel installed on your website (see Chapter 7 of this book)
2. A "thank you" page or any page that is on your website where someone lands after the event that would indicate the the conversion has happened. You can do button tracking as well, but that is beyond the scope of this book.

So for example, if you have someone signing up for a free ebook on your site you need to redirect them to a page on your website after they have completed signing up where the pixel is installed. That way Facebook knows the action has been completed and it can attribute that registration to that exact ad. My page https://www.andreavahl.com/50posts-thanks is where people land after they optin to get my free ebook about 50 Facebook Posts Guaranteed to Engage Your Audience. They can then download the free ebook right there.

Or if you have a form on your website where people contact you, you will need to then redirect them to a page that indicates the form has been filled out and the action is complete. If you have a store on your website, you can often track things like when people add a product to the cart and then make the purchase. A tool for creating an online store like Shopify can make this tracking process easy with the Facebook pixel.

You can't track Facebook ad conversions on other people's website (such as Amazon) because that site is not under your control. You are not able to put the pixel on their site.

Facebook's pixel has two ways you can track conversions:

- Standard Events
- Custom Conversions

The Standard Event method involves adding an extra bit of code ONLY on the pages where you are tracking a specific event (i.e. a "thank you" page).

The Custom Conversion method doesn't require any extra code added to the "thank you" pages; you just use a URL rule instead. This method is ideal for people that don't have many events to track and don't want the added hassle of adding the standard event code to their website.

USING THE CUSTOM CONVERSION METHOD (EASIER)

Because this book is called Facebook Ads Made Simple, I will only cover the easier method for tracking your Conversions. There are good reasons why you might want to use the Standard Event method but for now, let's go with the easy button!

Custom conversions allow you to track and optimize for conversions without adding any extra code to your site. All you need to know is the address of the web page that indicates the action is complete (i.e. the Thank You page).

To create a Custom Conversion follow these steps from your Ads Manager:

1. Select the three line menu icon in the upper left corner and then select Custom Conversions (you may have to select All Tools to see this option).

2. Select the **Create Custom Conversion button** in the upper right and a pop-up box appears. Now you need to configure your Custom Conversion.

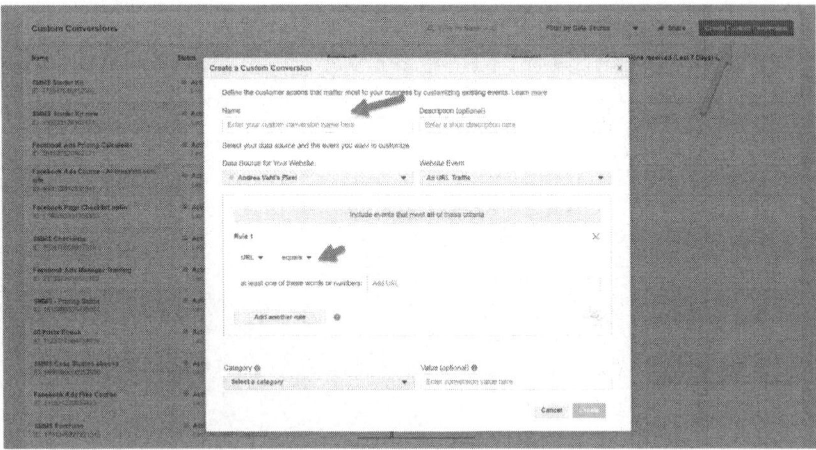

3. Give your Custom Conversion a name – make the name descriptive so you know exactly what the conversion represents. The Description is optional.

4. Add the rule you want to track. So if you are matching a particular page exactly, you enter that web address and use URL equals (make sure you include the www or http:// as needed). If you want to track across several types of pages you could use the URL contains /thankyou.php as an example if you had several 'thank you' pages that had that phrase in them. But be careful with

the "contains" option so you know that you are tracking the right things.

5. Select a category for your Custom Conversion. The Category isn't critical. Just choose something that resembles what is happening on your site when they land on this page.

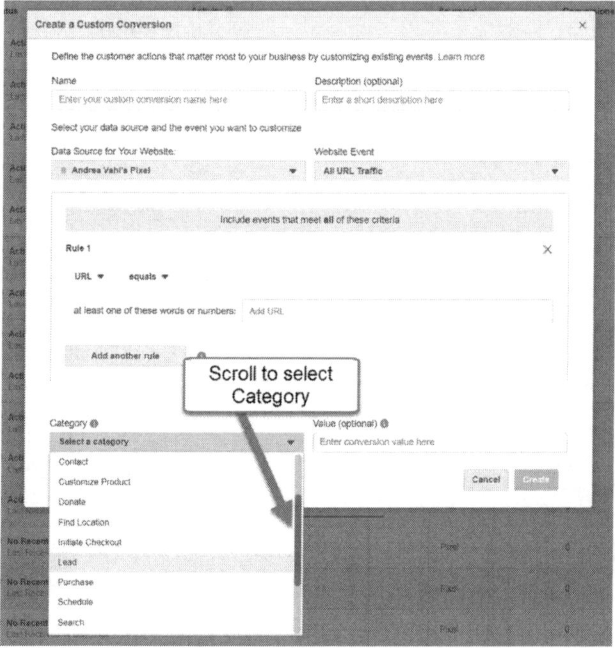

6. Add a conversion value if applicable (optional). This can be a good thing to do for items that been purchased or if you know how much a lead is worth to you.

7. Click Create to finish the process.

Now you will be able to use the Custom Conversion in ads and you will also see the traffic to the pages specified in those custom URL Rules on your Custom Conversions page.

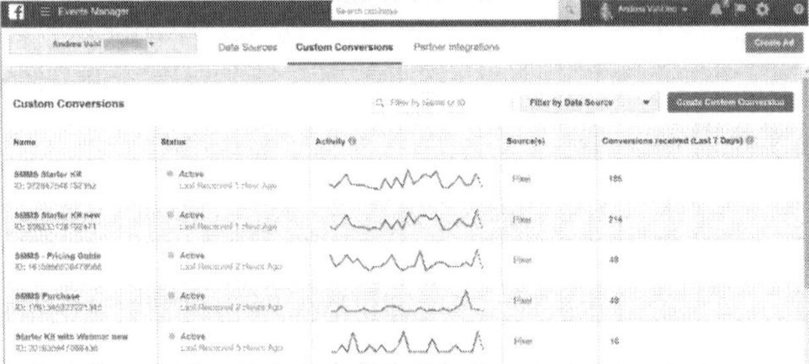

CREATING A CONVERSION AD

Now that you have your conversion method defined and your pixel installed, you are ready to track your conversions!

When you are in the Ads Manager area, click the Create Ad button is in the upper right corner to get started.

Then follow these steps:

1. Choose the Conversions selection. Note that you should ONLY use this selection if you already have the Facebook Pixel and your conversion method set up already.

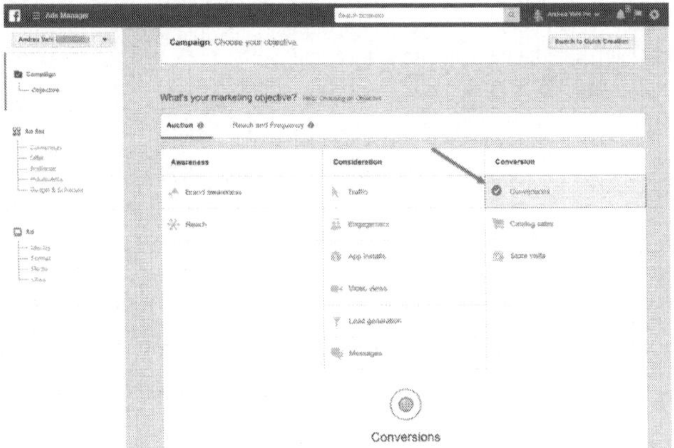

2. Name your Campaign and click Continue. Make sure you name your campaign something descriptive so that you will be able to easily read your reports.

3. At the Conversion section of the Ad Set, select the exact conversion you are optimizing around for this particular ad. Select the name of the Custom Conversion you just created.

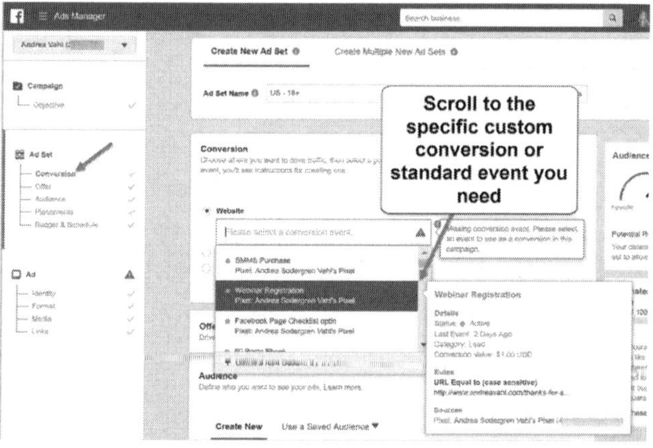

4. From here, you set up your ad exactly the same way you have done it in the past by selecting your targeting and budget in your Ad Set, and then move to setting up the creative part of your ad (image and text) at the Ad level.

5. Click Confirm in the lower right of the screen to start your ad running.

One thing to note is that your ad will automatically be set up to optimize for Conversions at the Ad Set level in the Budget & Schedule section. You can always change the bidding method, but your conversions will still be tracked. In general, it's best to keep the ad optimized around Conversions.

Also, note that you could create a Traffic Ad that would send people to the Landing Page but still track the Custom Conversions that came as a result of that Traffic Ad. If that sentence confuses you, do not worry—the point is that you are creating better ads now that you are tracking conversions!

WHAT YOU NEED TO RUN A LEAD GENERATION AD

Most advertisers I know are using Conversion ads rather than Lead Generation Ads. But if you don't have a website or if you want to test this Ad Objective out to see how it can work for your niche, it isn't too hard to set up.

In order to run a Lead Generation Ad you need a few things before you get started.

1. Design the Lead Form in the Publishing Tools area on your Facebook Page (or you can do this during the creation process in the Facebook Ads Manager). The Lead Form is the popup box that appears when someone clicks on your ad.
2. The system you will use to follow up with the leads. You can either have a link that will direct people to the Thank You page. Or you could manually email the people with the information they requested. Or you can set up some type of automation to automate the connection between the Publishing Tools area and your follow up system. Facebook has a number of integrations with tools like GetResponse, Marketo, GotoWebinar, ConvertKit, and many other systems. You can search to see if your system is available here:

https://www.facebook.com/business/help/908902042493I0
4. In some cases, it may be a 3rd party paid tool that you have to use to make the connection.

While you can create your Lead Form when you create your Ad, you may want to create it first so that you aren't holding up your ad creation process if you need something more.

To create your Lead Form, go to your Facebook Page and follow these steps:

1. Click Publishing Tools at the top of your Facebook Page.

2. Click Forms Library on the left sidebar. Any forms you have created for a Lead Generation ad in the past appear here.

3. Click the blue Create button on the left side of the Forms Library. A popup box appears to configure the form.

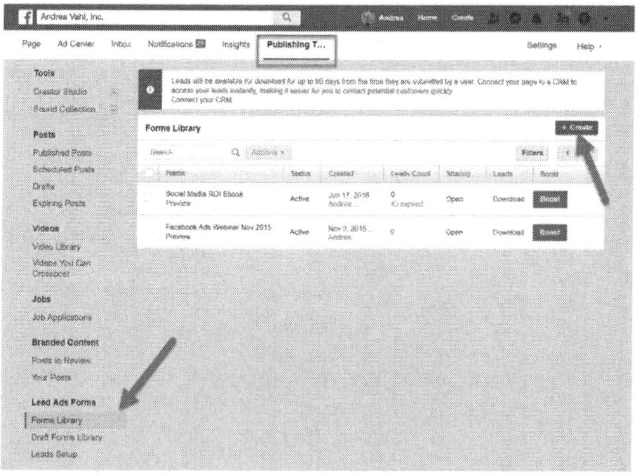

4. Name your form, add an image, and walk through each of the steps to configure your form. You do have to give a link to your

Privacy Policy in that section (which you should have on your website).

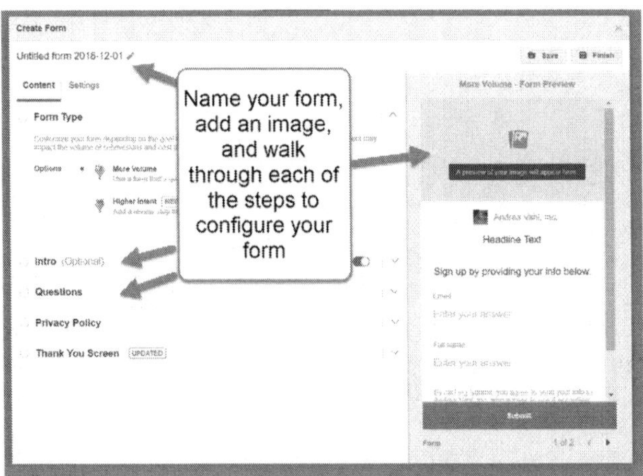

The most important section is the Questions, where you select what information you want from the person. Facebook pre-selects Full name and Email but you can customize what you ask for as well as customize the text in the form. Remember that the more information you ask for, the less likely that someone will give you their information.

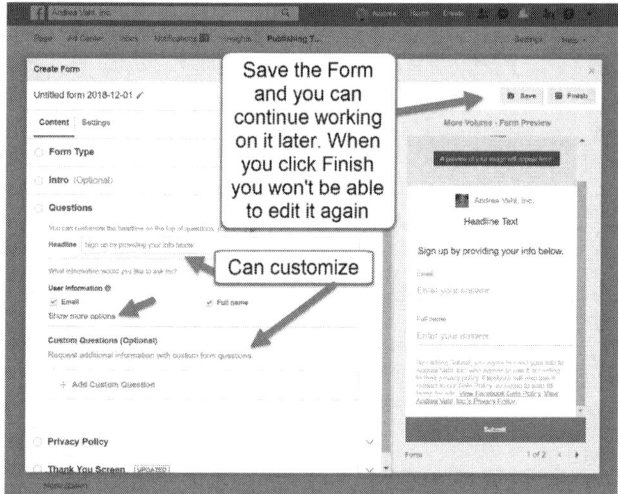

Once you are done creating the form, you can click Finish in the upper right corner and the Lead Form is ready to use in a Lead Generation Ad. But if you need to continue editing the Form later, select Save and the Form will be in Draft mode. You cannot use it in an Ad until you have clicked Finish.

CREATING A LEAD GENERATION AD

Now that you have created the Lead Form, all you need to do is create the Lead Generation Ad and specify that form in the Ad creation process. For the most part, creating the ad is just like creating any other ad, you'll use the same principles in targeting and writing your ad. There are a few differences in the process to highlight.

When you are in the Ads Manager area, click the Create Ad button is in the upper right corner to get started. Then follow these steps:

1. Choose the Lead Generation selection.

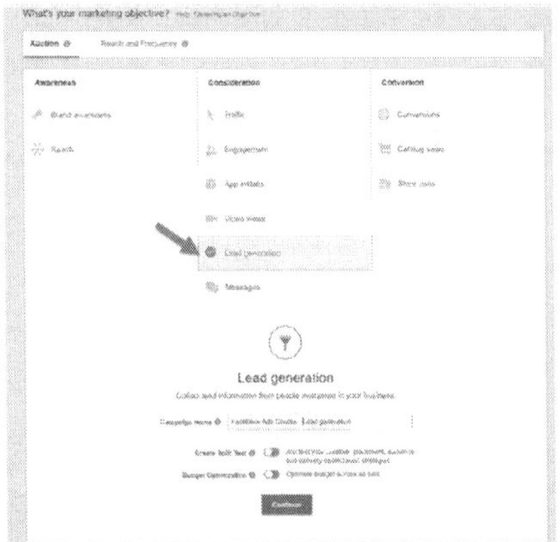

2. Name your Campaign and click Continue. Make sure you name your campaign something descriptive so that you will be able to easily read your reports.

3. At the Ad Set level, you will need to choose the Page you are promoting and accept the Lead Ad Terms if you haven't already.

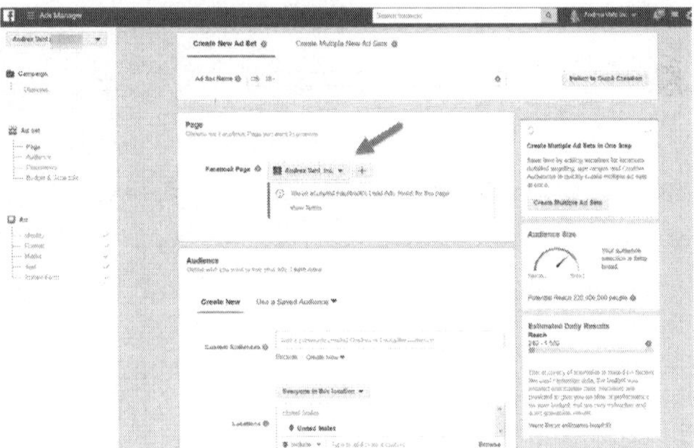

4. Now create your Ad Set just the same as before with the targeting, budgeting, placements, and settings you want to change.

5. When you move to the Ad level, you can create the Ad as normal but will select the Lead Generation Form (called the Instant Form here) for your lead capture. You will only see Forms that are in the "Finished" state, not draft forms.

6. Click Confirm to start your ad running.

Conversion ads and Lead Generation Ads take a little more setup time initially. But these types of ads are going to be better optimized to give you more leads and sales typically. Congratulations if you have set one of these types of ads up—you are well on your way to making the most of your Facebook Ads budget!

17

CUSTOM AUDIENCES AND RETARGETING

Custom Audiences (or just Audiences in the Ads Manager menu) are a big part of what makes Facebook ads so awesome. Custom Audiences give you the ability to reach your "warm" audience on Facebook—people who have been to your website, watched your videos, engaged with your Facebook Page, or signed up for your newsletter.

In this chapter, I will focus on how you Retarget your website visitors with a Facebook Ad. But you will also learn how to create some of the other Custom Audience options as well as Lookalike Audiences.

WHAT IS RETARGETING?

If you've ever been to Amazon and looked at a pair of pants, you may have noticed an ad for that pants following you all over the internet. That ad is "retargeting" you based on the fact that you looked at that item on their website. Now YOU get to be that pair of pants!

Retargeting is very effective because people often need to see your product or offer multiple times to make a buying decision. Some people worry that showing their ad over and over to people will be annoying. But if they have been to your website, they did show interest in your product or service. You can also watch the frequency of your ad. I don't want my frequency to get over 3-4 typically.

There are 3 steps to retarget your own website visitors with a Facebook ad:

1. Install the Facebook Pixel on your website
2. Create an Audience in your Facebook Ads Manager
3. Use that Audience in the Targeting section of your Facebook ad

Remember, you can install your pixel on multiple websites. This is helpful if, for example, you are using a service like Eventbrite for ticket sales or if you have multiple websites.

Hopefully, you have already accomplished step #1 from Chapter 7 in this book. So let's move on to step 2.

ACCESSING CUSTOM AUDIENCES

In the Audiences section, you can create Saved Audiences, Custom Audiences, and Lookalike Audiences. Here are some brief definitions of what each of these mean:

- Custom Audience – Email subscribers, Website Retargeting, Facebook App Activity, Engagement on Facebook
- Lookalike Audience – A group of Facebook profiles that are "similar" to one of your Custom Audiences
- Saved Audience – Targeting that you save to use again to save you time

To get to the Audiences section, go to the hamburger menu in the upper left corner from your Facebook Ads Manager and select Audiences.

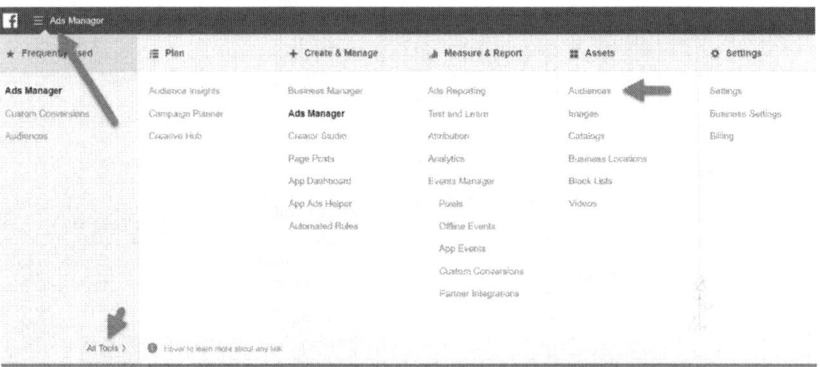

The Audiences screen includes all the Custom, Saved, and Lookalike Audiences you may have created. Initially, there are no audiences there and you are prompted to create some audiences. But if you have already created audiences, you will see them listed in the columns area along with Type, Size, and Availability.

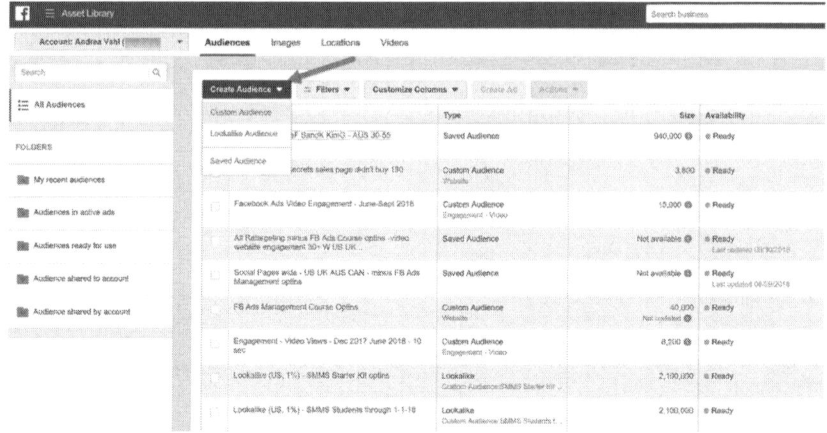

To create new Audiences, you use the dropdown menu accessed by clicking on Create Audience. When you click Custom Audience, you see a popup box with all types of options. I definitely suggest creating multiple types of these audiences. But in this chapter we will focus on Retargeting.

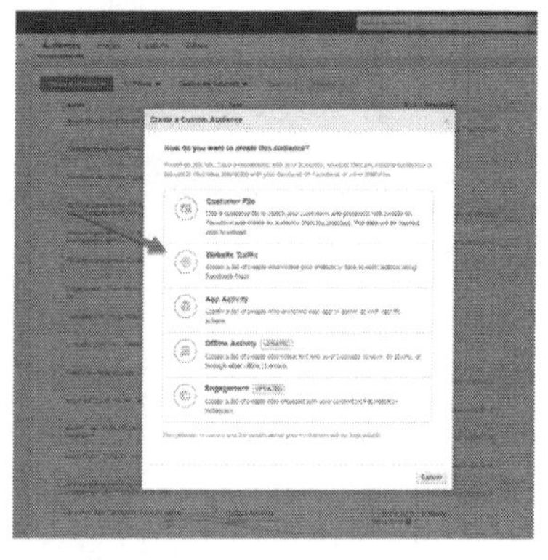

The Website Traffic audience will be the one that retargets people who have been to your website. The other Audiences valuable to most businesses are Engagement and Customer File. The Customer File audience requires that you move your Page and your Ads Manager into Business Manager which is covered in the next chapter.

CREATING YOUR CUSTOM AUDIENCE FOR RETARGETING

Because each Facebook Ads account just gets one pixel and the pixel can be placed on multiple websites, you need to tell Facebook which Website Traffic you want to use and "retarget."

When you select Website Traffic from the popup box shown previously, you will see another popup box where you configure your Custom Audience by using the dropdown menu that appears when you click All website visitors.

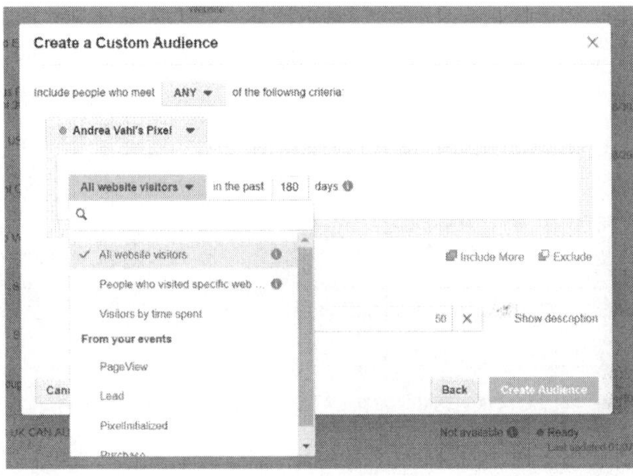

You can choose anyone who has visited any website you have the pixel installed on within the last 180 days (from the time you installed the pixel and that is the maximum time frame). This is the perfect "first audience" to create because it is the most open.

You can also choose specific web pages, which means you can choose a particular domain or even a specific page on your whole website. And you can create complex combinations.

For example, you could choose people who had visited a sales page but not visited the thank you page (people who hadn't converted). Or you could choose to create an audience of anyone who had visited particular pages on your website related to the same thing and target them with a specific offer.

You also want to name your audience appropriately so that you know what it is when you select it in your Targeting section. For example, I would name this audience "All website traffic - 180 days." If I created an audience that was just to a certain sales page or product page in the last 30 days, I would name it "XYZ sales page - 30 Days".

After you create the Audience, it does take some time to populate and be ready for use. So create your Audience a minimum of a day before you use it.

Some things to know about Website Audiences:

- The time frame is a rolling period. So if you choose 30 days, it's the most recent 30 day time period
- 180 Days is the maximum time period you can target
- The Website Audience auto updates so you don't have to recreate it ever again
- You can use any Custom Audience in Boosted Posts or through the Ads Manager

The biggest limitation is that the audience will need to be large enough to target in an ad campaign – which is typically around 1000 people but can be smaller. Facebook doesn't reveal the exact number. Sneaky Facebook.

They will indicate that your Audience is too small if it's very small in the "Availability" column by showing a Red dot and a "Not

Available" message. A lot of business owners just don't get enough traffic to particular web pages to target them individually.

LOOKALIKE AUDIENCES AND SAVED AUDIENCES

The two other types of options in the Audiences section are Lookalike Audiences and Saved Audiences.

A Lookalike Audience can be a very powerful tool for having Facebook go out and "find" similar people to your customers, your email subscribers, your Fans, or website visitors. That way you aren't having to figure out the right keywords to target—Facebook is doing the work for you.

A Lookalike Audience basically takes any Custom Audience as the "seed" to go out and find Facebook profiles like that audience. Some ideas for good Lookalike Audiences to create are:

- Similar audience to your Page
- Similar audience to your Subscribers and customers
- Similar audience to your Website visitors

Or more advanced Lookalike Audiences:

- Lookalike of customers who have bought multiple products
- Lookalike of people who spend a certain duration of time on your site
- Lookalike of email subscribers who open multiple emails

The size of the Lookalike Audience that Facebook creates depends on the country you choose (you can only narrow your audience by country - you can restrict it further in the Targeting section of the Facebook Ad).

To create a Lookalike Audience, follow these steps from the Audiences screen:

1. Click the Create Audience and select Lookalike Audience from the dropdown menu. A popup box appears.

2. Click the Source box to select the source of your Audience. You can select other Custom Audiences you have created, Pages, Apps or the whole Pixel. Click Other sources to see the Custom Audiences.

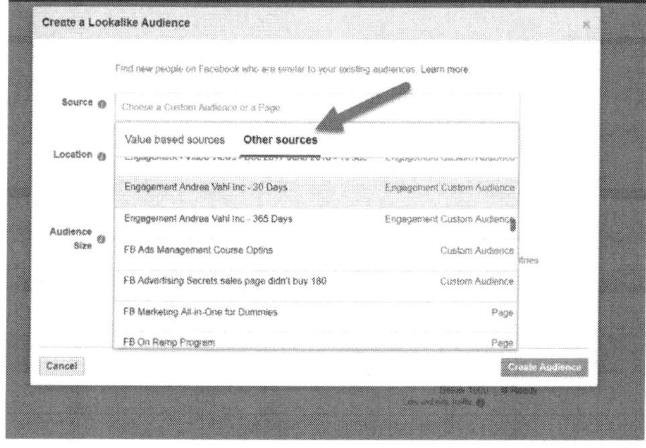

3. Select the Country and the Size of the audience you want to create.

4. The Size will be based on the country, and I like to keep the size typically in the smallest range by electing one country at a time. You can combine Lookalike Audiences in the Targeting section of Facebook Ads.

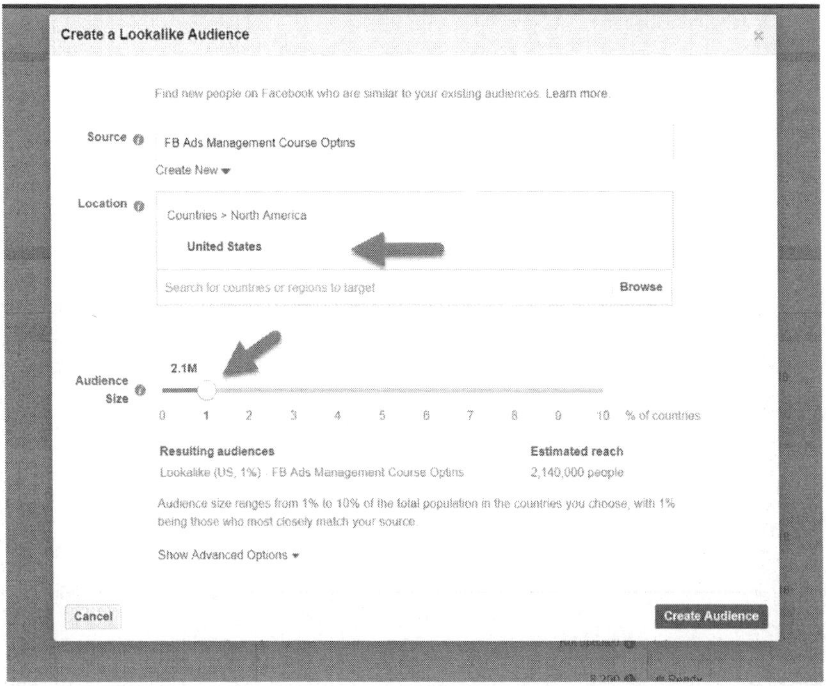

Lookalike Audiences require testing as with ANY type of audience. I sometimes find they don't convert as well as when I choose my targeting specifically but they can also do well for different niches. Sorry I don't have a sweeping generalization of an answer but you know what you need to do - TEST!

A Saved Audience basically allows you to save time by saving your targeting for audiences that have worked well for you in the past. You can create your Saved Audience in the Ad creation process or in the Audiences section. When you go to create a Saved Audience, the interface looks exactly like the Targeting section at the Ad Set level except that you have to title your Saved Audience.

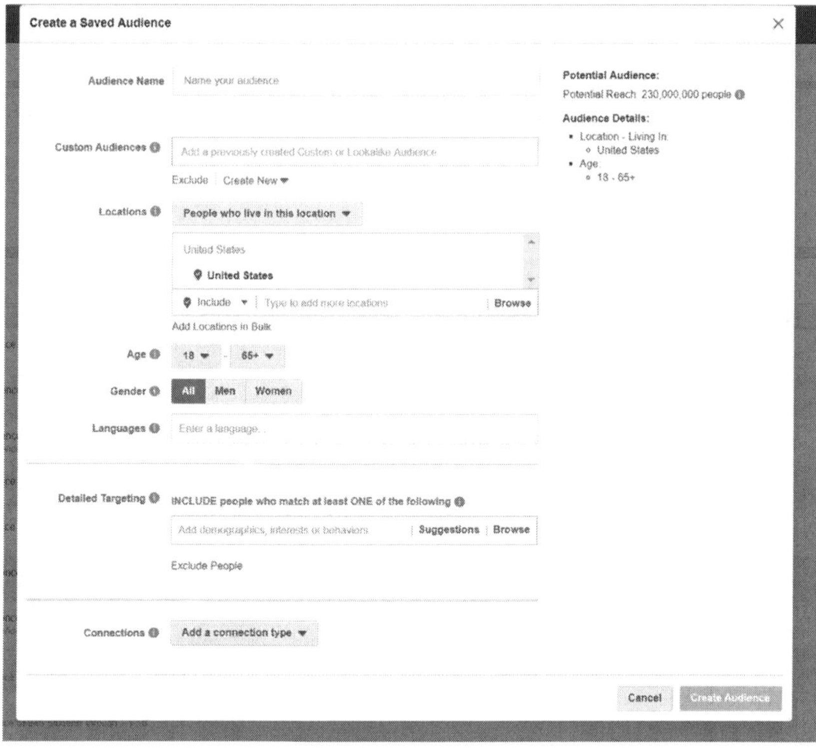

I do encourage you to only Save audiences that you know work for you so you don't get confused when choosing audiences.

USING THE CUSTOM AUDIENCE IN AN AD

Once you have created an Audience, then you need to use the Audience in an ad. When you select an Audience, you are telling Facebook to only show your ad to the people in that Audience. So often, that targeting will be much smaller since you are only showing your ad to the people who have visited your website.

In order to target the Audience in an ad, start creating your ad and then in the Audience section, then select the Custom Audience you created earlier from the Custom Audiences box. It's important to name your Audiences well so that you can easily choose the right audience.

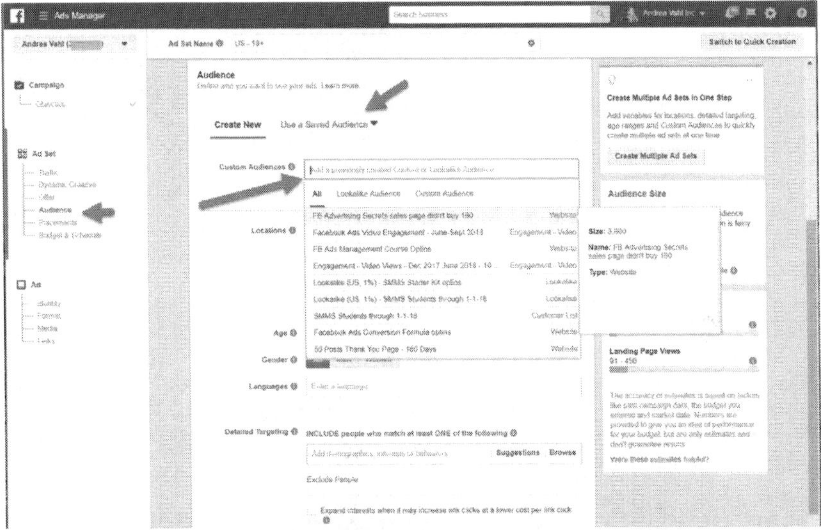

I don't recommend putting any other targeting keywords on a Website Audience because you want to reach anyone in that audience typically. But Lookalike Audiences could possibly use some demographic targeting to narrow them down just a little. Click on the Use a Saved Audience to access those.

You can also use your Custom Audiences in a Boosted Post. Just navigate to the Custom Audience selection and choose which one to target in your Boosted Post.

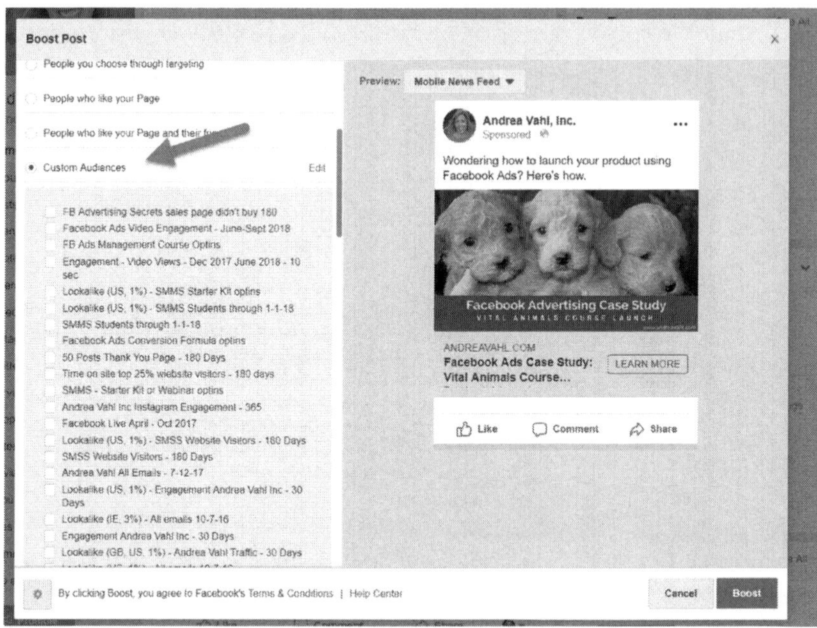

One of the biggest pitfalls of Custom Audiences and Retargeting is that you can't target a small audience. One of the ways around this is to combine Audiences. You can select multiple Custom Audiences to target in your Ad.

You can select all your Facebook Fans, all your Website visitors, and all the people who have watched at least 10 seconds of your recent videos for example. Then that combined audience might be over 1000 people and you can target that group.

Another thing to note but something that is very positive is that when you are targeting a small audience, you don't have to spend that much to reach them. People often tell me that they see my ads all the time on Facebook. I'm actually not spending THAT much on a monthly basis. I just retarget my warm audience with my blog posts.

Retargeting saves you money because you don't have to spend that much to reach that highly targeting audience.

We are only scratching the surface with Custom Audiences and I go much more in depth in my full Facebook Advertising Secrets course here: hhttps://fbadvertisingsecrets.com/opennow. You get online videos, training, and downloadable resources as well as one-year access to a private Facebook Group where you can ask me questions! Priceless!

GREAT TIP FROM FOXWELL DIGITAL

"If you ask a dozen different Facebook advertising experts how to properly scale accounts, you'll no doubt receive a dozen different answers. Scaling effectively doesn't follow an easy-to-follow recipe. But if you're someone who enjoys multivariate testing, monitoring campaigns closely, and moving potential customers along your sales funnel in creative ways, scaling will be very rewarding. You're also probably super nerdy like we are! That said, if you're someone looking for a "set it and forget it" plan, scaling will prove difficult and tiresome. Scaling techniques change frequently and with just a minor algorithmic shift, your ads can quickly turn to dust after performing perfectly the day before. To help you better understand scaling, let's look at the difference between vertical and horizontal scaling before providing a couple of common scenarios.

Vertical vs. Horizontal Scaling

To scale successfully and sustainably, you can't just increase your budget, leave it, and see amazing results. This method of scaling, also known as vertical scaling, depends entirely on the budget being the only lever you can pull for improved ROI. Instead of using only one lever, we prefer to utilize horizontal scaling. In this case, an advertiser spreads testing across multiple ad sets, audiences, and types of creative with the overall purpose of building a more stable account structure for long-term, scalable success. So let's dive in with a couple recommendations that you can use right away.

Scenario #1: Scaling a Lookalike

Problem: *"I have an ad set targeting a lookalike of my previous customers that's performing well with more than a 2X return on ad spend (ROAS) and I want to grow it. What options do I have?"*

Solution: *Try launching ads to two new lookalike audiences based on pixel events. You can group them into one ad set or separate them, depending on the amount of audience overlap between them. Most advertisers test a 1% lookalike of previous customers as their first prospecting audience. This is a great start, but as a next step try building lookalike audiences from pixel events. Customer lists work well, but pixel events are dynamic, meaning the core audience updates in real time and the lookalike audience regenerates every 3-7 days.*

Scenario #2: Avoiding High Frequency

Problem: *"People tell me I'm bombarding them with ads. I have Website Custom Audience remarketing ads set up for anyone who has come to my site in the last 90 days. It has done well and produced a 3X ROAS in the past, but the frequencies are above 10 and performance is going down. What should I do?"*

Solution: *Most advertisers have a super simple remarketing program running on autopilot. They need a more sophisticated approach. Keep in mind that if you saw something 14 times in 30 days, would that encourage you to buy it? That level of frequency would most often lead to annoyance. So in most cases, the mistake that's being made is lumping all remarketing traffic into one ad set with the same pitch going to the same group. If you visited a website 90 days ago and you're seeing the same message as someone who came to the site yesterday, this is clearly a problem.*

Andrew and Gracie Foxwell, Co-Founders, Foxwell Digital, FoxwellDigital.com

Andrew and Gracie specialize in E-commerce ads and have run ads for Pura Vida, Kind, GoPro, Hootsuite, Blenders Eyewear and all kinds of other amazing companies - and they are both super cool people to hang out with.

18

USING THE BUSINESS MANAGER

Have you heard about Facebook's Business Manager and just want it explained to you in simple terms? Should you be using the Facebook Business Manager? When don't you need to use it?

I feel like with a title of "Business Manager," this tool should do more than it really does. Shouldn't it be helping me out by making decisions for me, or at least doing my taxes? Sadly, no.

There are a lot of misconceptions about the Business Manager. In this chapter you will learn when you should use it, how to get started using it, and some of the pitfalls with using it. You may already be using it, so some of the navigation in the earlier part of the book didn't make as much sense. Facebook is actually forcing the move to Business Manager for many Page owners so sooner or later we will all probably have to use it.

WHAT IS THE FACEBOOK BUSINESS MANAGER?

The Facebook Business Manager is just another way to access Pages and Advertising Accounts. Facebook released the Business Manager in 2014; its main purpose is to make Pages and Ad Accounts easier and more secure to work on for teams of people.

Think of it as an "umbrella" that the Page and the Ad Account live under.

You can easily give different people on your team different levels of access to each Facebook Page or Ads Account in your management portfolio. The Pages,Ads Manager, and Power Editor all function the same once you access those areas. **The Business Manager is just a central hub for managing the accounts.**

Some people don't realize they migrated to the Business Manager —you can tell for sure if you navigate to your Page and there is a gray bar at the top with Business Manager name. The website address when you work in Business Manager will be https://business.facebook.com.

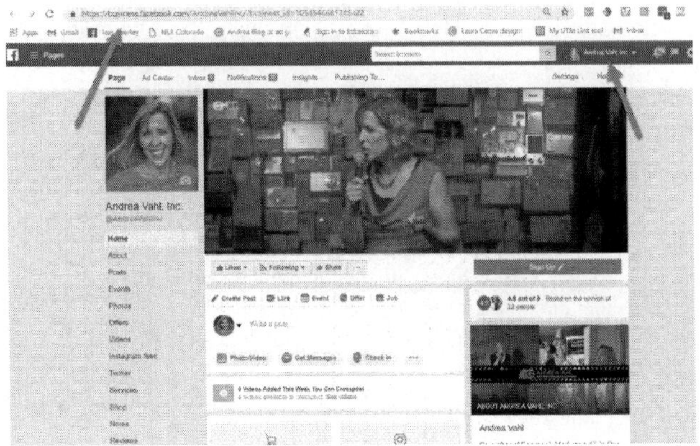

When you navigate to the Business Manager area, your initial screen is different. You will see all the Pages or Ads Accounts that you have access to on the main page. You can have multiple Ad accounts under one Business Manager and multiple Pages.

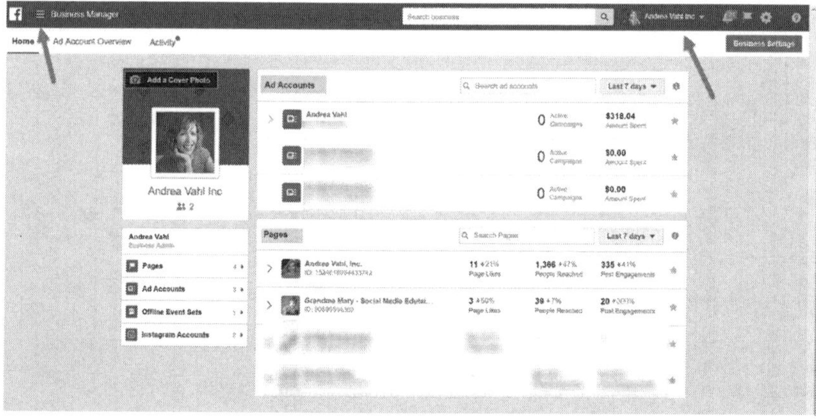

Each person in a Business Manager account will only see the assets that they have been given access to. You can have multiple people inside each Business Manager account and assign different levels of access to each of them.

But once you navigate to the Facebook Page or the Ads Manager, everything about those spaces are EXACTLY the same. **All the processes for working on your ads and creating ads in the Ads Manager are the same.** Posting on your Page is the same and accessing the Page Insights is the same. The ONLY difference is the initial navigation and how you give people permission to work on your Page or Ads Manager.

To start creating an Ad in the Ads Manager, all you need to do is to click on the name of the Ad Account on this main Business

Manager dashboard page. Then you can begin the process of creating the ad exactly as you would have before.

WHEN DO YOU NEED THE FACEBOOK BUSINESS MANAGER?

The Facebook Business Manager is best when you have a **team of people** working on multiple Pages or Ad Accounts. So think **agencies or larger businesses with multiple admins.**

If you are a smaller business with one Facebook Page and one Facebook Ads account, you can have multiple admins to those accounts but you still may want to have a central place to control permissions.

Also note that if you are going to have an agency or person help you post on your Page or run your Ads, **you DON'T need to switch to Business Manager just because they are using it.** You can just give them access to your Page and Ads Manager. That way they can access your Page and use the Business Manager.

One recent development is that Facebook is **now requiring people to switch to the Business Manager to continue using the Customer Lists within Custom Audiences.**

The ONLY part of the Custom Audiences that are currently affected by this change are the Customer File Audiences. These are the emails or phone number you may have uploaded into the Audiences section.

BUT I do think Facebook is making a push for all Page owners to eventually migrate to Business Manager (in fact, many Page owners have seen Facebook force this switch during the writing of this book). So we may all be making this switch sooner rather than later.

One advantage to Business Manager is you can create multiple Ads Managers (up to 5) under one Business Manager, which allows you to keep accounts separated and have separate billing on each Ad Account.

3 ESSENTIAL STEPS TO USING THE FACEBOOK BUSINESS MANAGER

Just to be super clear on what it takes to use Facebook Business Manager after you get the initial creation done, you will need to complete these steps. Facebook's setup process guides you a bit in these steps but not perfectly.

1. Add Pages and Ads Accounts – Only claim Pages or accounts that you own (you can also create a brand new Ads account if you don't use one already).
2. Add People – You are already added if you created the Business Manager. But if you have other people on your team that need access, you will have to invite them to your Business Manager. They will get a notification to join.
3. Assign People to the Assets that they are allowed to work on – Once the people have joined, you can then assign the assets that they can access.

These steps can all be done in the initial setup or from the Business Settings Page (either the blue button in the upper right corner or navigate to the menu item from the upper left corner hamburger menu).

THINGS TO KNOW BEFORE YOU GET STARTED WITH BUSINESS MANAGER

There are some key points that are good to understand before using Business Manager.

1. It's generally best when the true "owner" of the company starts the process of forming the Business Manager for the company but someone else can create the Business Manager for you. Then that person can give the proper Admin access to other members of the team.
2. There is a big difference between **Claiming Assets** and **Requesting Access to Assets.** If you need to work on someone else's Page or Ads account, you should Request Access to those assets and not claim them.
3. If you CLAIM an Ad Account, it is very difficult to remove that ad account from the Business Manager – hopefully Facebook will adjust that.
4. Once you move a Page into the Business Manager, you will have to use the Facebook Pages App to access the Page on mobile devices.
5. Business Managers can work together and give access to another Business Manager under the Partners section of the Business Settings.
6. When you add people into your Business Manager, they will get an email invitation to join and no other notification (more on this later in the chapter).

The steps you take to move into Business Manager are fairly straightforward - first you create the Business Manager and then you move your Page and your Ads Manager into the Business Manager.

GETTING STARTED WITH THE BUSINESS MANAGER

Some accounts have been prompted to migrate to the Business Manager and may have a message in their Ads Account area. But the easiest way to migrate to Business Manager is to go directly to https://business.facebook.com/ and scroll down to the Get Started Button.

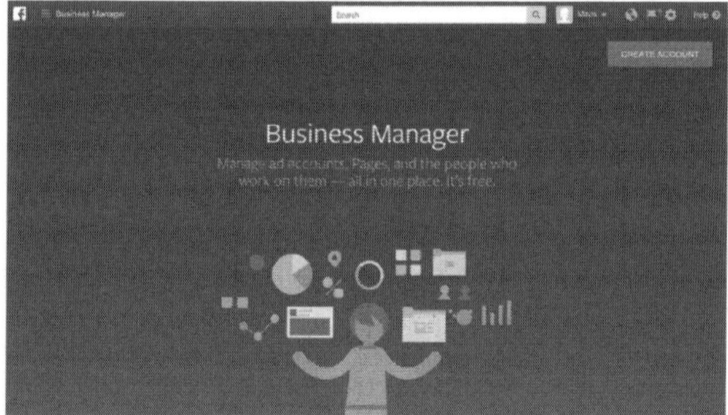

Once you click the blue Create Account button, you'll see a pop-up box with just 2 steps to getting started.

STEP 1

The first step is to just name your Business Manager account. It can be the same name as your Page. Just know that they will both have the same name when you are navigating around. No one will see this name—t's for your internal use only. Then add your own name and the email you will use for your Business Manager. You can use a different email or the same one you use to log into your personal profile if you want.

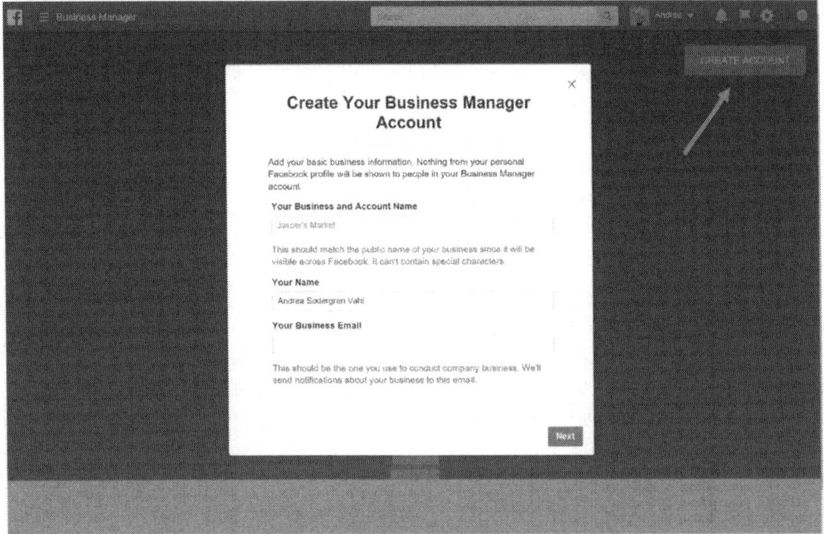

STEP 2

The second step is to add your Business Details. You can't skip this step so even if you don't have a traditional "Business Address," you do have to add an address and website here.

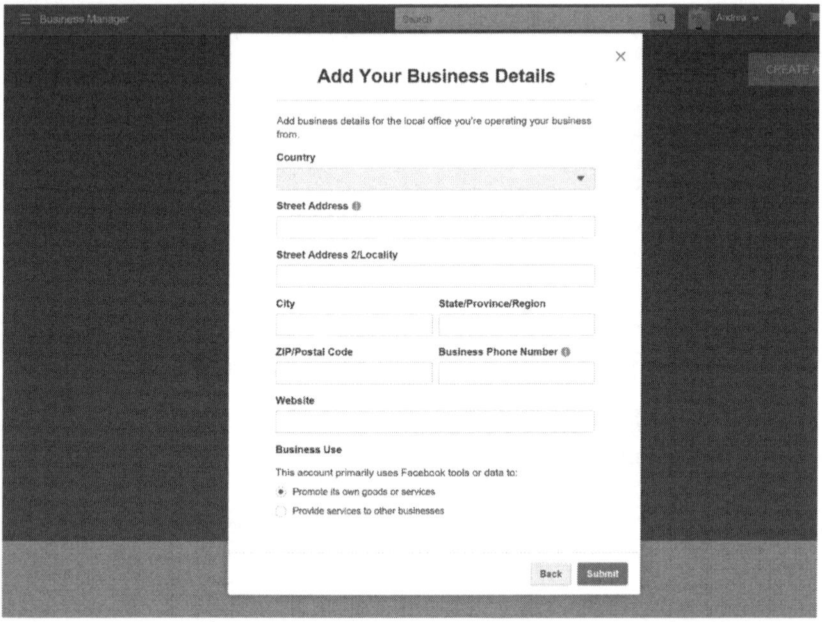

STEP 3

After you get set up, they will send a verification email to your email you listed but you can start setting up your new Business Manager by adding Pages, Ad Accounts, and People. You can do those steps from this screen but you can also add assets to the Business Manager in the Business Settings section.

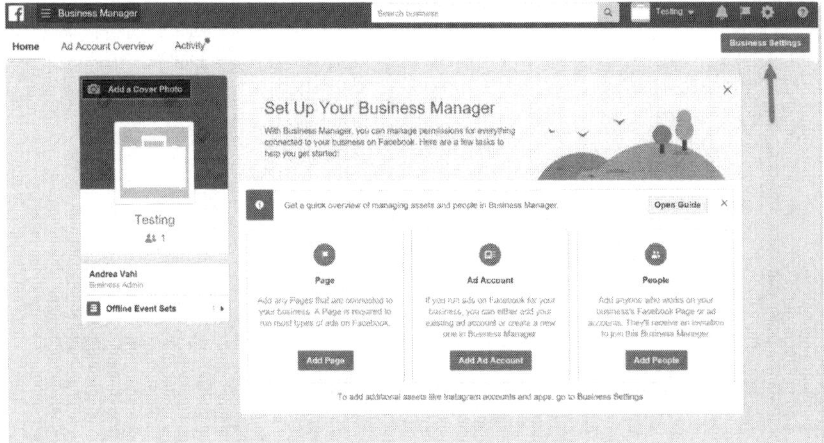

Facebook now makes the difference between adding your own Ads Manager and Requesting access to another Ads Manager much clearer when you click the Add an Ad Account on this initial setup.

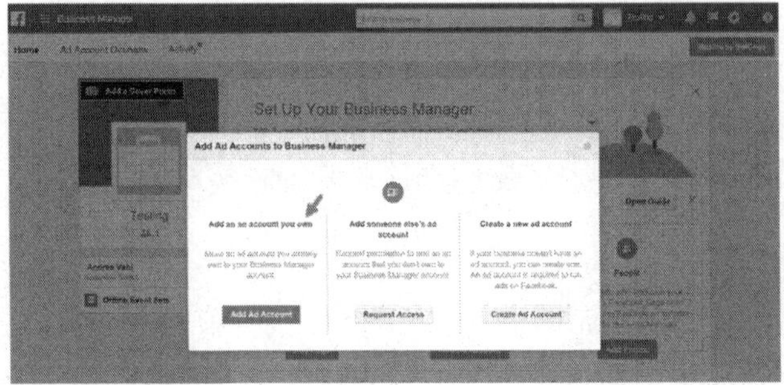

You can also go to the Business Settings area (click on the blue Business Settings button in the upper right corner) and add new People, Pages, or Ad Accounts.

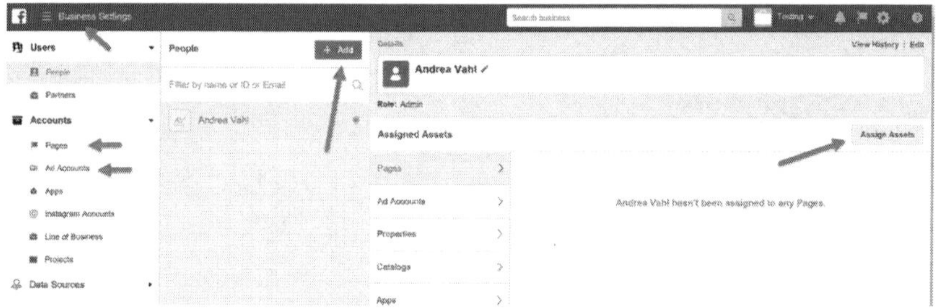

If you are Adding an Ad Account, you will have to know the Ad account ID. This can be found inside your Ads Manager in the upper left corner and will also be part of the URL when you are in your Ads Manager.

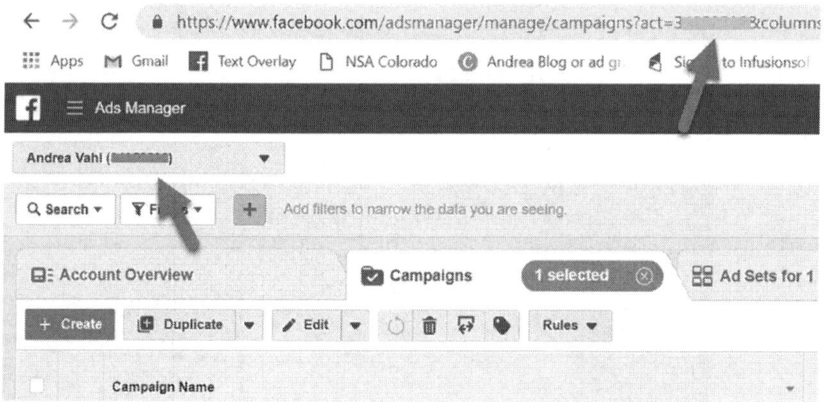

To add your Ad Account to your Business Manager, follow these steps:

1. From the Business Settings area, click Ad Accounts on the left sidebar.

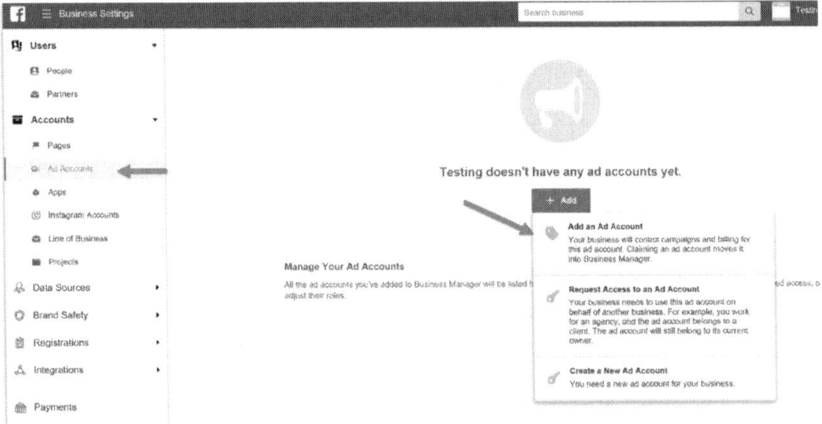

2. Click the blue Add button. Select Add an Ad Account from the dropdown menu that appears.

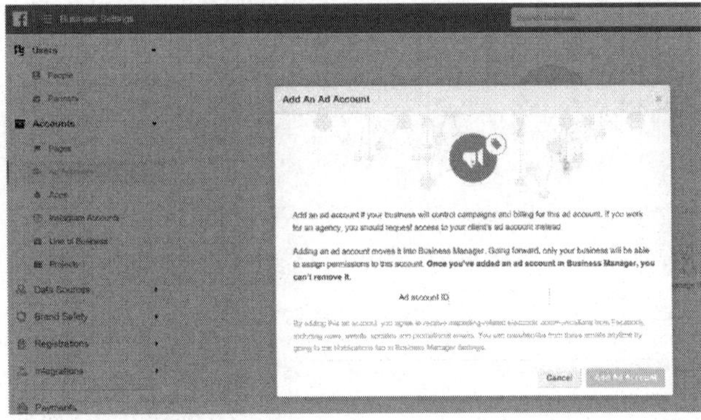

3. Add your Ad account ID number in the popup box that appears and select the blue Add Ad Account button.

Claiming an Ads Account (a.k.a. Adding an Ad Account) cannot be undone as far as I can see, so be very careful about claiming Ads Accounts. You can always **request access** to another Ads Account, and the owner of that Ads Account will retain the information about the ads and stats. This would be appropriate if you are running ads on behalf of a client or a business.

More on the 3 options (directly from Facebook here: https://www.facebook.com/business/help/530540643805698)

- Add an Ad Account: Adding an ad account moves it permanently into Business Manager. You must be both the owner of the ad account and an admin in Business Manager to do this. Please note: Once you add an ad account and it's moved into your Business Manager, this action can't be reversed. All management of your ad account must be completed within your Business Manager profile. You can't add an ad account that's owned by another Business Manager. If you still want to work on an ad account that's owned by a different business, you can request access to it.
- Request Access to an Ad Account: If you request access to an ad account in Business Manager, the admin of that Business Manager can grant you permission to work on it.
- Create a new ad account: If you create a new ad account in Business Manager it'll permanently belong to that Business Manager. Once created within Business Manager, the ad account can't be transferred to an individual owner who doesn't own a Business Manager.

If you can't add an ad account to a Business Manager, check their troubleshooting hints at the above link.

ADDING PEOPLE TO YOUR BUSINESS MANAGER AND ASSIGNING ASSETS

To Add New People to your account, you can do that from the initial setup screen when you create your Business Manager or from the Business Settings area by selecting the People option from the left sidebar then by clicking Add New.

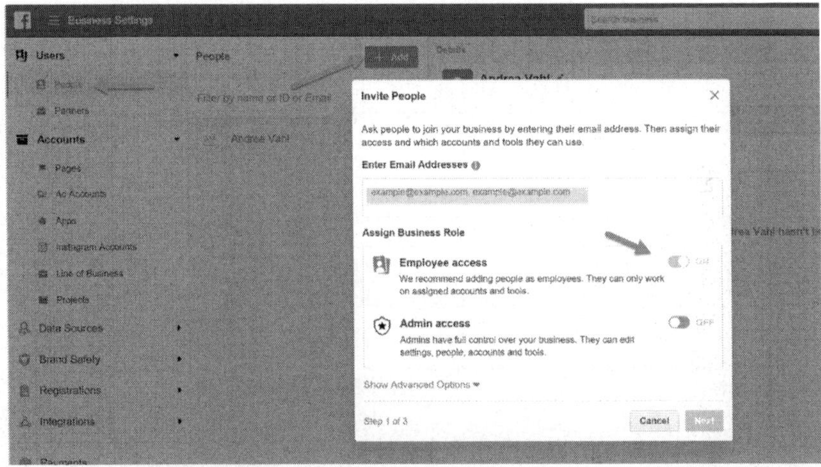

Add people at the "Employee" level even if they aren't a true employee of yours. Reserve Admin access for a few main people or just yourself, as Admins have the ability to delete accounts or remove other Admins.

Facebook will then prompt you to assign assets to the people you have added. But if you miss that step, you can always assign assets in the People section after you have added them.

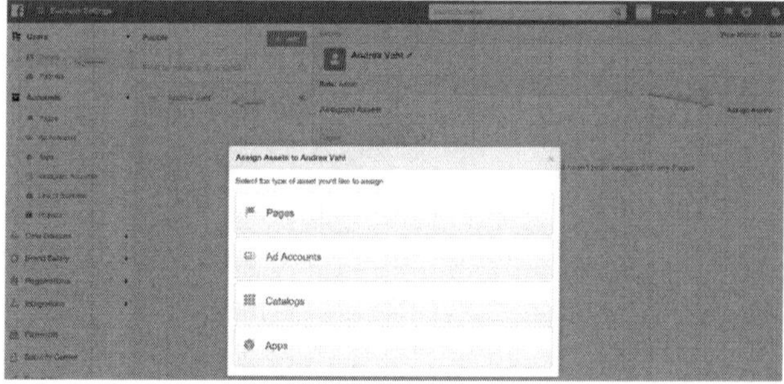

In order for the person to work on your Page or Ads Account, they will need to accept the invitation to your Business Manager.

CONFIRMING YOUR INVITATION TO THE BUSINESS MANAGER

If you have been invited to a Business Manager, you will receive an email from Facebook (mine goes into my "Social" tab automatically because I use Gmail) The subject line is "_Pagename_ has invited you to work on their business on Facebook"

The person will need to confirm that they want to be added to that Business Manager by clicking the Get Started button in their email. This invitation can be resent from the Business Setting section.

Then they will need to create a name and e-mail that they will use to log in. It's fine to use the current email they use to log into Facebook, but they can use a business email if preferred.

You can also remove people from your Business Manager that no longer need access.

I think the Business Manager is perfect for larger teams and agencies. It is also much safer for

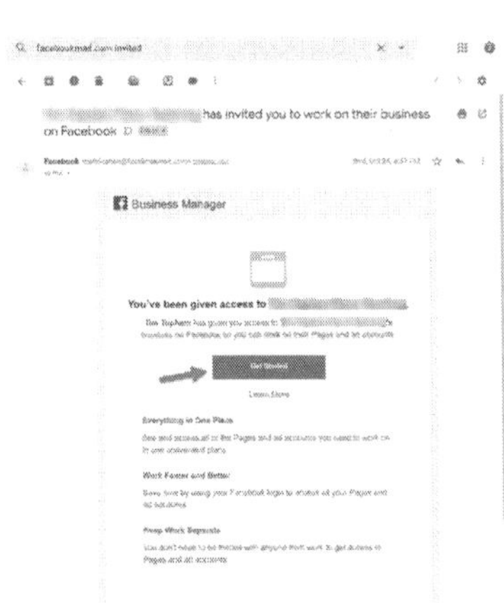

protecting Pages if people have unique logins to the Business Manager. It might feel a little scary when you are setting it up, but once you have it set up, it is basically the same as using the Ads Manager and your Page like you did before.

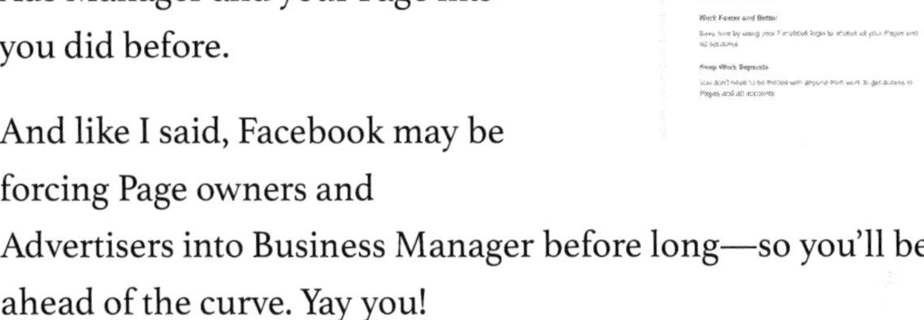

And like I said, Facebook may be forcing Page owners and Advertisers into Business Manager before long—so you'll be ahead of the curve. Yay you!

CONCLUSION

Wooohooooo!!! You made it, smarty pants! Not only are you smarter now, but you are also going to save more money on your Facebook Ad Campaigns which makes you extra smart.

FINAL TAKEAWAYS

I know we've covered a LOT in this book. But let me try and distill everything into a couple of bite-sized recommendations.

#1 - TEST!

If you haven't gotten the message yet, Facebook Ad success really comes down to testing. If you aren't seeing the results you want from an ad after 4-5 days (and at least $50 in budget), then continue to split test. Again, this depends a little bit on your niche. But the more you continue to test, the more information you will have on what works best for you.

#2 - FOCUS FUTURE ADS ON CONVERSIONS IF POSSIBLE

We started off with a Traffic ad in this book because that is simplest. But Facebook Ads work better overall if you can use the Pixel and focus on Conversions. Facebook learns what types of people convert in your market and can optimize to show your ads to the right audience.

Facebook continues to improve their own capabilities in finding new ways to improve their offering in the Facebook Ads tactics. They are constantly working on optimizing their ads to help advertisers be more successful. Many people think Facebook is just out to make a buck (and I know I tell my share of jokes, too). But the advertisers are what continue to fund their business. Facebook wants you to be successful.

#3 - ALWAYS BE LEARNING

Facebook changes constantly - okay, I know I'm preaching to the choir with that statement - so you need to continue to keep on top of what is working and what's new. I don't test every single new thing that comes out right away. I often wait a little bit to see how it shakes out and then run some tests.

You also have to circle back to things you may have already tested in the past because sometimes the feature gets better or Facebook changes how the algorithm works. Keep an open mind and keep wise counsel.

If you haven't yet signed up for my email newsletter (you are on my email list if you signed up for the book resources), you can do that on my blog: www.andreavahl.com/blog. I also give a lot of tips and Facebook Ads news on my Facebook Page: www.facebook.com/AndreaVahlinc.

#4 - FIND A FACEBOOK ADS SUPPORT GROUP

Getting feedback and having a sounding board is priceless when you are running Facebook Ads. Facebook can be quirky (understatement of the year) and new things are changing all the time in the Ads Manager.

If you want to really dive deep into Facebook Ads and get a year of online support in my private Facebook Group, you can join my Facebook Advertising Secrets course at https://fbadvertisingsecrets.com/opennow.

This course has 2 levels - one for any type of business looking to learn how to use Facebook ads to grow their business (the Basic

Level), and then also a level for people who want to build a business running Facebook Ads for clients (the Agency level). I only open the course a few times a year so you can visit the page and get on the waiting list (plus get a free Facebook Ads mini-course).

#5 YOU CAN OUTSOURCE YOUR ADS MANAGEMENT BUT UNDERSTAND THE BASICS

There are lots of great Facebook Ads consultants and agencies out there. I've trained amazing people through my Facebook Ads Secrets Course with my Agency level training. BUT there are also some not so great consultants out there who talk in circles to confuse their customers and don't do a good job with ads.

It's best to know how Facebook Ads work and some of the terms so that you aren't getting bad information. Get referrals from people who have worked with a trained consultant or agency.

BEYOND THE BOOK - CONTINUED RESOURCES!

Make sure you have signed up for the FREE walk through video and other resources that will help with this book at www.andreavahl.com/book-resources. Here, I do a live demo of setting up an ad from scratch and give you pointers along the way of settings you can to change and what you can ignore. Plus, I show you EXACTLY how to create the ad in an hour or less. :)

Thanks so much for starting your Facebook Ads journey with me!

I appreciate you taking the time to invest in your success and learn a new skill. I know it can be uncomfortable to learn a new skill but I hope this book made it SIMPLE for you! I would love it if you left an Amazon Review for this book. Feel free to send me a message on my Facebook Page to let me know what you thought. You've got this - I'm cheering for you!

ACKNOWLEDGMENTS

I want to especially thank my family who supported me and encouraged me through this process — Steve, Devin, and Henry — you guys are my heroes. And my mastermind group who helped with ideas, suggestions and feedback — Pamela Wilson, Karyn Greenstreet, Henneke Duistermaat, and Julie Smith. Thanks for keeping me somewhat sane.

I also want to especially acknowledge some of my early friends and mentors who made a HUGE difference in where I am today because of their connection, the chance they took on me, and their example of where you can go in this world. Phyllis Khare for giving me the original connection to *Facebook Marketing All-in-One for Dummies,* our co-author Amy Porterfield who connected me to Social Media Examiner, and Mike Stelzner who I worked with at SME. I wouldn't be where I am without all of you. And Sonia Simone who grew a great early support system for me called the Remarkables — thank you for all your wisdom.

ABOUT THE AUTHOR

Andrea Vahl is a Social Media Speaker and Consultant who is passionate about helping businesses understand and leverage the power of Facebook Ads to actually grow their business. Andrea is the co-author of *Facebook Marketing All-in-One for Dummies* and was the Community Manager for Social Media Examiner, for over 2 years.

She has appeared in top lists on Entrepreneur.com and Inc.com and speaks and trains all over the world. She is the co-founder of Social Media Manager School an online learning program with over 1500 students. Andrea Vahl's proven ability to make social media marketing easy to understand and implement has directly impacted the bottom line of thousands of companies through her training and one-on-one consulting. She is also a stand up comedienne. Learn more about Andrea's books, courses, and resources, on her website, www.AndreaVahl.com.

facebook.com/AndreaVahlinc

twitter.com/AndreaVahl

instagram.com/andreavahl

youtube.com/andreavahl

amazon.com/author/andreavahl

Made in the USA
Columbia, SC
13 November 2020